TRUTH STRANGER
THAN FICTION

Slave narratives

- roots
- native son
- uncle Toms cabin

3 types
Colonial (early 1800's)
Antibellum (1820 - before the civil war) "how I achieved freedom"
Postbellum (after the civil war) "how I achieved success"

antibellum slave Narratives

- mostly by men
- modelded on Douglas
- Physical and spiritual enslavement
- Personal voice
- focus on escape to the north
- Continouse and heavy brutality
- critical of democracy
- confused / lost parentage
- literacy

you cant as a slave "man up"
- cant be independent
- cant take responsibility
- have to be free to be a man

more christian identity than Douglass
retorical style (sentimentality)

◆ THE BARNES & NOBLE LIBRARY OF ESSENTIAL READING ◆

TRUTH STRANGER THAN FICTION
Father Henson's Story of His Own Life

JOSIAH HENSON

INTRODUCTION BY ERIC ASHLEY HAIRSTON

BARNES & NOBLE
NEW YORK

THE BARNES & NOBLE
LIBRARY OF ESSENTIAL READING

Introduction and Suggested Reading
© 2008 by Barnes & Noble, Inc.

Originally published in 1858

This 2008 edition published by Barnes & Noble, Inc.

Barnes & Noble, Inc.
122 Fifth Avenue
New York, NY 10011

ISBN: 978-1-4351-0838-7

Printed and bound in the United States of America

1 3 5 7 9 10 8 6 4 2

Contents

INTRODUCTION

TRUTH STRANGER THAN FICTION: FATHER HENSON'S STORY OF HIS OWN LIFE
stands as a remarkable narrative on its own merits, but even more
significant is its relationship to one of the most celebrated anti-slavery
tracts in American literature and one of its controversial characters.
Josiah Henson's life story is noted as a source for the character of
Uncle Tom in Harriet Beecher Stowe's *Uncle Tom's Cabin*.[1] It is strange
that an inspiration for Stowe's character, who has been a touchstone
for complicated cultural criticism and whose name is a contemporary
curse, should be based on an escaped slave, one-time soldier, preacher,
founder of an independent black settlement, and slave-narrative
writer. More telling is how starkly Henson's narrative illustrates the
troubling literary license taken by Stowe and how sentimentalist aboli-
tionist texts of the era achieved pathos by simplifying and to some
extent emasculating actual black men like Josiah Henson in order to
attain palatable characters for white audiences. In truth, Henson
struggled mightily to rise to the top of the slave hierarchy, gain the
trust of his masters on merit, and meet them as brothers in Christ,
only to be bitterly disappointed and find that there was neither merit
nor reward for his work and no honor, honesty, trust, compassion, or
Christian charity in his Southern masters and overseers. Unlike
Stowe's derivative character, Henson seized his freedom, made a life
for himself in Canada, and freed fellow slaves before publishing his
life story and taking the cause of the slaves and fugitives to England
and before Queen Victoria herself.

[handwritten margin notes: tolerable / tasteful / non-threatening]

Born in 1789 in what is now North Bethesda, Maryland, Josiah
Henson saw his father maimed and beaten for opposing the attempted
rape of his mother, driven into depression, and later sold South to
Alabama. Henson was himself separated from his mother and then, on
the brink of death, sold for a pittance to the doctor who had purchased his mother and would later give him his name. During his
youth, Henson labored to obtain privilege within the slave system,
eventually caused the dismissal of an overseer, and assumed the position himself—endeavoring to skim additional sustenance for his slave
brethren as his position grew. Henson was converted to Christianity at
the age of eighteen, and by 1828, although still enslaved, he became a
preacher in the Methodist Episcopal Church. In 1830, stunned by his
various slaveholders' deceptions and ingratitude (even after saving
their lives on a number of occasions) and fearful for the welfare of his
family, he embarked with his wife and children on a perilous escape
to Canada. After remarkable adventures involving Quakers and Native
American assistance, Henson reached Canada and a new life. Active in
the Underground Railroad, Henson returned to the United States
and brought more than a hundred fellow slaves to Canada. There he
tutored fugitive slaves in agricultural production and marketing, mov-
ing in 1842 to his project community, the fugitive settlement of Dawn,
with its manual-labor school for blacks. As a result of his lumbering
project in Dawn, Henson traveled to England to seek debt relief and
exhibit the productions of fugitive slaves at the 1851 Great Exhibition.
His display caught the attention of Queen Victoria, who later sent a
medal and photograph of the royal family to Henson, who counted
them among his prize possessions. Henson returned to Canada in
1852, to attend to his dying wife. Soon after, he met Harriet Beecher
Stowe in Massachusetts and spoke with her at length about his life
story, which had already appeared in print by 1849. He claimed to
know many of the sources for the characters in *Uncle Tom's Cabin*,
including George Harris, who W. J. Hartgrove notes in his 1918 article
in *The Journal of Negro History*, was actually named Lewis Clark and
traveled and lectured with Henson on many occasions.[2] Stowe herself
referred to Clark as a friend and source in *The Key to Uncle Tom's
Cabin* (1854). Henson served as an officer in a company of "colored

volunteers" during the 1837 Canadian Rebellion in defense of his adopted country. In his waning years, Henson was able to travel for a third time to England, where he was again greeted in audience by Queen Victoria. He returned to the United States to visit his old plantation haunts and to be received by President Rutherford B. Hayes. Henson continued his work in Canada during his later years, where he died in 1883 at the age of ninety-four.

Henson' narrative might not have achieved the broad notoriety of other narratives, like Frederick Douglass' 1845 *Narrative of the Life of Frederick Douglass,* and its absolute veracity has been challenged. However, as Mary Ellen Doyle noted decades ago, a remarkable portion of the narrative can be verified by its references to specific names, events, and occasions that have independent records of their own, as well as contemporary sources like *The Liberator.*[3]

The narrative begins with a faithful celebration of his wondrous deliverance from the suffering of slavery. Like the biblical Daniel, he has survived a furnace of troubles and been tempered by God in the process. Just after the reader settles comfortably into the deceptive sense of religious rapture, Henson's pious comparison to Old Testament heroes quickly gives way to the hellish realities of slavery. The reader is rapidly plunged into the world of blood and barbarism, learning in only few pages that one of the narrator's first memories is of his incensed father, nursing a bloody head and raw, whipped back—the battle wounds of having defended his mother against an attempted rape by an overseer. Henson balances the crime of rape against the crime of "a nigger [striking] a white man" and shows that the scale of nineteenth-century justice is completely unbalanced. Moreover, the crime of striking a white man exceeds mere law to reach a kind of pure sacrilege, a corruption that the Christian Henson is careful to note. While rape was the prerogative of white slaveholders, injuring the "sacred temple of a white man's body [was] a profanity as blasphemous in the slave-state tribunal as was" the entry of a Gentile dog into the Holy of Holies. In short order, Henson drives home his opening point with bloody precision. The price of defending the virtue of a black woman in the Old South is clear—one hundred lashes, one's ear nailed to a post, and the same ear sliced off.

It is this juxtaposition of the slaveholder law and slaveholder religion against the justice and faith of civilized men and women that underpins and structures the intellectual architecture of Henson's autobiography. In this he is as deliberate in his writing as Frederick Douglass, leaving the reader little room to justify, accommodate, or excuse slavery. He paints a picture of a slave culture maintained in large part by a combination of alcohol, ignorance, and mob justice and immune to the appeals of manhood, womanhood, motherhood, or religion. Not content to dwell just on the American atrocity, he quickly connects the politics and horrors of American slavery to a broader global process of colonialism and imperialism. In a deft move that has even twenty-first-century resonance, he reminds his own contemporary readers not to be quick to disbelieve the fundamental viciousness of white culture in Maryland when in their own day they could "find tender English women and Christian English divines fiercely urging that India should be made one pool of Sepoy blood."

For Henson, the degradation of slaveholding society extended even to those slaveholders who exhibited "kind impulses" and measures of religious conviction. The relatively benign slaveholder who gave Henson his own Christian name was found drowned in less than a foot of water, the ultimate result of a long dissipation by revels and alcoholism. In a scene remarkably common to slave narratives and slave poetry, the dissolution of his owner's estate wrenched families apart, including his own, and unleashed misery above even that daily experienced in an enslaved existence. Henson's principal adventures began after he watched his mother literally kicked away from him by slave-traders.

Henson's narrative shares features with many others of the era, including a focus on the brutality of the daily operations of slavery and plantation life, a recollection of hideous treatment of slaves and especially of women, meditations on the essential barbarism of slaveholder culture, and comparisons of true Christian faith and the adulterated faith of slaveholding society. Henson also faces life-altering experiences that eventually lead him to seize his manhood and his freedom. His trip down the Mississippi is a surreal and dark journey, an inversion of the playful and liberating trips down the river later provided by Mark Twain and so embedded in the American psyche. Unlike

Frederick Douglass, who bests Edward Covey to assert his manhood, Henson has a slightly more disparate and complex experience. He exposes the embezzlement of one overseer and takes the position himself. But, he is later ambushed and maimed for life by an overseer from another plantation in revenge for having defended his drunken master in a brawl against several white opponents. While slaves like Solomon Northup remained relatively humble in their narratives, Henson rivals Frederick Douglass in burnishing his own manhood and accomplishment. Successive editions of the narrative expand and embellish his service on behalf of the Dawn settlement and his travels to England and America to be received by notables. His prowess as a minister and leader of fugitive slaves also becomes more pronounced and luminous as the narrative expands across its various editions. A Prince Hall Mason during his lifetime, Henson's exploits have been observed as part of a significant relationship between early ideas of African-American masculinity and the ritual formation of identity in the Masonic Order.[4]

Today Henson is still remembered in Canada and the United States. The Dawn Settlement Cabin in Ontario and the Montgomery County, Maryland, slave cabin that housed Henson are both intact. The Ontario Heritage Society operates a well-developed historic site in Ontario that includes Henson's House titled as "Uncle Tom's Cabin," outbuildings, an underground railroad home, and the Henson family cemetery. A museum and gallery also accompany the historic buildings. Montgomery County acquired the Maryland slave cabin in 2006 with plans to eventually open it to the public.

In its own time, Josiah Henson's narrative occupied a place in a literary landscape increasingly populated by narratives and dominated by the life story of Frederick Douglass. For contemporary readers, Henson's account possesses the notable quality of providing a representative account of one of the more than fifty thousand slaves who escaped across the border to Canada. Henson was careful to note that one of the reasons for his expanded narrative was the request from many readers that he include some account of the lives of fugitive slaves in Canada, and this Afro-Canadian perspective is a necessary and significant addition to the broader story of the Atlantic slave trade. Henson's narrative is an excellent complement to the more widely celebrated texts in the slave-narrative genre. Today the various editions of Henson's narrative receive light to moderate scholarly attention, a benign neglect that hopefully will be remedied by scholars looking beyond the more popular narratives.

Eric Ashley Hairston is an Assistant Professor of English and of Law and Humanities at Elon University. He holds a Ph.D. in English Language and Literature from the University of Virginia, as well as a J.D. from the University of North Carolina at Chapel Hill. He teaches and writes on American literature, African-American literature, Western literary history, Classical literature, Asian-American Literature, and Law and Humanities.

PREFACE

THE NUMEROUS FRIENDS OF THE AUTHOR OF THIS LITTLE WORK WILL need no greater recommendation than his name to make it welcome. Among all the singular and interesting records to which the institution of American slavery has given rise, we know of none more striking, more characteristic and instructive, than that of JOSIAH HENSON.

Born a slave—a slave in effect in a heathen land—and under a heathen master, he grew up without Christian light or knowledge, and like the Gentiles spoken of by St. Paul, "without the law did by nature the things that are written in the law." One sermon, one offer of salvation by Christ, was sufficient for him, as for the Ethiopian eunuch, to make him at once a believer from the heart and a preacher of Jesus.

To the great Christian doctrine of forgiveness of enemies and the returning of good for evil, he was by God's grace made a faithful witness, under circumstances that try men's souls and make us all who read it say, "lead us not into such temptation." We earnestly commend this portion of his narrative to those who, under much smaller temptations, think themselves entitled to render evil for evil.

The African race appear as yet to have been companions only of the sufferings of Christ. In the melancholy scene of his death—while Europe in the person of the Roman delivered him unto death, and Asia in the person of the Jew clamored for his execution—Africa was represented in the person of Simon the Cyrenean, who came patiently bearing after him the load of the cross; and ever since then poor

Africa has been toiling on, bearing the weary cross of contempt and oppression after Jesus. But they who suffer with him shall also reign; and when the unwritten annals of slavery shall appear in the judgment, many Simons who have gone meekly bearing their cross after Jesus to unknown graves, shall rise to thrones and crowns! Verily a day shall come when he shall appear for these his hidden ones, and then "many that are last shall be first, and the first shall be last."

Our excellent friend has prepared this edition of his works for the purpose of redeeming from slavery a beloved brother, who has groaned for many years under the yoke of a hard master. Whoever would help Jesus, were he sick or in prison, may help him now in the person of these his little ones, his afflicted and suffering children. The work is commended to the kind offices of all who love our Lord Jesus Christ in sincerity.

H. B. Stowe
Andover, Mass., April 5, 1858

CHAPTER ONE

MY BIRTH AND CHILDHOOD

Earliest memories • Born in Maryland • My father's first appearance • Attempted outrage on my mother • My father's fight with an overseer • One hundred stripes and his ear cut off • Throws away his banjo and becomes morose • Sold South

THE STORY OF MY LIFE, WHICH I AM ABOUT TO RECORD, IS ONE FULL OF striking incident. Keener pangs, deeper joys, more singular vicissitudes, few have been led in God's providence to experience. As I look back on it through the vista of more than sixty years, and scene on scene it rises before me, an ever fresh wonder fills my mind. I delight to recall it. I dwell on it as did the Jews on the marvellous history of their rescue from the bondage of Egypt. Time has touched with its mellowing fingers its sterner features. The sufferings of the past are now like a dream, and the enduring lessons left behind make me to praise God that my soul has been tempered by him in so fiery a furnace and under such heavy blows.

I was born June 15th, 1789, in Charles County, Maryland, on a farm belonging to Mr. Francis Newman, about a mile from Port Tobacco. My mother was a slave of Dr. Josiah McPherson, but hired to the Mr. Newman to whom my father belonged. The only incident I can remember which occurred while my mother continued on Mr. Newman's farm, was the appearance one day of my father with his head bloody and his back lacerated. He was beside himself with mingled rage and suffering. The explanation I picked up from the conversation of others only partially explained the matter to my mind; but as

1

I grew older I understood it all. It seemed the overseer had sent my mother away from the other field hands to a retired place, and after trying persuasion in vain, had resorted to force to accomplish a brutal purpose. Her screams aroused my father at his distant work, and running up, he found his wife struggling with the man. Furious at the sight, he sprung upon him like a tiger. In a moment the overseer was down, and, mastered by rage, my father would have killed him but for the entreaties of my mother, and the overseer's own promise that nothing should ever be said of the matter. The promise was kept— like most promises of the cowardly and debased—as long as the danger lasted.

The laws of slave states provide means and opportunities for revenge so ample, that miscreants like him never fail to improve them. "A nigger has struck a white man"; that is enough to set a whole county on fire; no question is asked about the provocation. The authorities were soon in pursuit of my father. The fact of the sacrilegious act of lifting a hand against the sacred temple of a white man's body—a profanity as blasphemous in the eye of a slave state tribunal as was among the Jews the entrance of a Gentile dog into the Holy of Holies—this was all it was necessary to establish. And the penalty followed: one hundred lashes on the bare back, and to have the right ear nailed to the whipping-post, and then severed from the body. For a time my father kept out of the way, hiding in the woods, and at night venturing into some cabin in search of food. But at length the strict watch set baffled all his efforts. His supplies cut off, he was fairly starved out, and compelled by hunger to come back and give himself up.

The day for the execution of the penalty was appointed. The negroes from the neighboring plantations were summoned, for their moral improvement, to witness the scene. A powerful blacksmith named Hewes laid on the stripes. Fifty were given, during which the cries of my father might be heard a mile, and then a pause ensued. True, he had struck a white man, but as valuable property he must not be damaged. Judicious men felt his pulse. Oh! He could stand the whole. Again and again the thong fell on his lacerated back. His cries grew fainter and fainter, till a feeble groan was the only response to the final blows. His head was then thrust against the post, and his right ear fastened to it with a tack; a swift pass of a knife, and the bleeding member was left sticking to the place. Then came a hurra from the degraded crowd, and the exclamation, "That's what he's got for striking a white man." A few said, "it's a damned shame"; but the majority regarded it as but a proper tribute to their offended majesty.

It may be difficult for you, reader, to comprehend such brutality, and in the name of humanity you may protest against the truth of these statements. To you, such cruelty inflicted on a man seems fiendish. Ay, on a *man;* there hinges the whole. In the estimation of the illiterate, besotted poor whites who constituted the witnesses of such scenes in Charles County, Maryland, the man who did not feel rage enough at hearing of "a nigger" striking a white to be ready to burn him alive, was only fit to be lynched out of the neighborhood. A blow at one white man is a blow at all; is the muttering and upheaving of volcanic fires, which underlie and threaten to burst forth and utterly consume the whole social fabric. Terror is the fiercest nurse of cruelty. And when, in this our day, you find tender English women and Christian English divines fiercely urging that India should be made one pool of Sepoy blood, pause a moment before you lightly refuse to believe in the existence of such ferocious passions in the breasts of tyrannical and cowardly slave-drivers.

Previous to this affair my father, from all I can learn, had been a good-humored and lighthearted man, the ringleader in all fun at corn-huskings and Christmas buffoonery. His banjo was the life of the farm, and all night long at a merrymaking would he play on it while the other negroes danced. But from this hour he became utterly changed. Sullen, morose, and dogged, nothing could be done with him. The milk of human kindness in his heart was turned to gall. He brooded over his wrongs. No fear or threats of being sold to the far south—the greatest of all terrors to the Maryland slave—would render him tractable. So off he was sent to Alabama. What was his after fate neither my mother nor I have ever learned; the great day will reveal all. This was the first chapter in my history.

CHAPTER TWO

MY FIRST GREAT TRIAL

Origin of my name • A kind master • He is drowned • My mother's
prayers • A slave auction • Torn from my mother • Severe
sickness • A cruel master • Sold again and restored to my mother

AFTER THE SALE OF MY FATHER BY NEWMAN, DR. MCPHERSON WOULD
no longer hire out my mother to him. She returned, accordingly, to his
estate. He was far kinder to his slaves than the planters generally were,
never suffering them to be struck by anyone. He was a man of good,
kind impulses, liberal, jovial, hearty. No degree of arbitrary power
could ever lead him to cruelty. As the first negro-child ever born to
him, I was his especial pet. He gave me his own Christian name, Josiah,
and with that he also gave me my last name, Henson, after an uncle of
his, who was an officer in the Revolutionary war. A bright spot in my
childhood was my residence with him—bright, but, alas! Fleeting.
Events were rapidly maturing which were to change the whole aspect
of my life. The kind Doctor was not exempt from that failing which too
often besets easy, social natures in a dissipated community. He could
not restrain his convivial propensities. Although he maintained a high
reputation for goodness of heart and an almost saint-like benevolence,
the habit of intemperance steadily gained ground, and finally occasioned his death. Two negroes on the plantation found him one
morning lying dead in the middle of a narrow stream, not a foot in
depth. He had been away the night previous at a social party, and when

returning home had fallen from his horse, probably, and being too intoxicated to stagger through the stream, fell and was drowned. "There's the place where massa got drownded at"; how well I remember having it pointed out to me in those very words.

For two or three years my mother and her young family of six children had resided on this estate; and we had been in the main very happy. She was a good mother to us, a woman of deep piety, anxious above all things to touch our hearts with a sense of religion. How or where she acquired her knowledge of God, or her acquaintance with the Lord's Prayer, which she so frequently taught us to repeat, I am unable to say. I remember seeing her often on her knees, trying to arrange her thoughts in prayer appropriate to her situation, but which amounted to little more than constant ejaculations, and the repetition of short phrases which were within my infant comprehension, and have remained in my memory to this hour.

Our term of happy union as one family was now, alas! At an end. Mournful as was the Doctor's death to his friends it was a far greater calamity to us. The estate and the slaves must be sold and the proceeds divided among the heirs. We were but property—not a mother, and the children God had given her.

Common as are slave-auctions in the southern states, and naturally as a slave may look forward to the time when he will be put up on the block, still the full misery of the event—of the scenes which precede and succeed it—is never understood till the actual experience comes. The first sad announcement that the sale is to be; the knowledge that all ties of the past are to be sundered; the frantic terror at the idea of being sent "down south"; the almost certainty that one member of a family will be torn from another; the anxious scanning of purchasers' faces; the agony at parting, often forever, with husband, wife, child— these must be seen and felt to be fully understood. Young as I was then, the iron entered into my soul. The remembrance of the breaking up of McPherson's estate is photographed in its minutest features in my mind. The crowd collected round the stand, the huddling group of negroes, the examination of muscle, teeth, the exhibition of agility, the look of the auctioneer, the agony of my mother—I can shut my eyes and see them all.

My brothers and sisters were bid off first, and one by one, while my mother, paralyzed by grief, held me by the hand. Her turn came, and she was bought by Isaac Riley of Montgomery county. Then I was offered to the assembled purchasers. My mother, half distracted with the thought of parting forever from all her children, pushed through the crowd, while the bidding for me was going on, to the spot where Riley was standing. She fell at his feet, and clung to his knees, entreating him in tones that a mother only could command, to buy her *baby* as well as herself, and spare to her one, at least, of her little ones. Will it, can it be believed that this man, thus appealed to, was capable not merely of turning a deaf ear to her supplication, but of disengaging himself from her with such violent blows and kicks, as to reduce her to the necessity of creeping out of his reach, and mingling the groan of bodily suffering with the sob of a breaking heart? As she crawled away from the brutal man I heard her sob out, "Oh, Lord Jesus, how long, how long shall I suffer this way!" I must have been then between five and six years old. I seem to see and hear my poor weeping mother now. This was one of my earliest observations of men; an experience which I only shared with thousands of my race, the bitterness of which to any individual who suffers it cannot be diminished by the frequency of its recurrence, while it is dark enough to overshadow the whole afterlife with something blacker than a funeral pall.

I was bought by a stranger named Robb, and truly a robber he was to me. He took me to his home, about forty miles distant, and put me into his negro quarters with about forty others, of all ages, colors, and conditions, all strangers to me. Of course nobody cared for me. The slaves were brutalized by this degradation, and had no sympathy for me. I soon fell sick, and lay for some days almost dead on the ground. Sometimes a slave would give me a piece of corn bread or a bit of herring. Finally I became so feeble that I could not move. This, however, was fortunate for me; for in the course of a few weeks Robb met Riley, who had bought my mother, and offered to sell me to him cheap. Riley said he was afraid "the little devil would die," and he did not want to buy a "dead nigger"; but he agreed, finally, to pay a small sum for me in horse-shoeing if I lived, and nothing if I died. Robb was a tavern keeper, and owned a line of stages with the horses, and lived near Montgomery courthouse; Riley carried on blacksmithing about five miles from that place. This clenched the bargain, and I was soon sent to my mother. A blessed change it was. I had been lying on a lot of rags thrown on a dirt floor. All day long I had been left alone, crying for water, crying for mother; the slaves, who all left at daylight, when they returned, caring nothing for me. Now, I was once more with my best friend on earth, and under her care; destitute as she was of the proper means of nursing me, I recovered my health, and grew to be an uncommonly vigorous boy and man.

The character of Riley, the master whom I faithfully served for many years, is by no means an uncommon one in any part of the world; the evil is, that a domestic institution should anywhere put it in the power of such a one to tyrannize over his fellow beings, and inflict so much needless misery as is sure to be inflicted by such a man in such a position. Coarse and vulgar in his habits, unprincipled and cruel in his general deportment, and especially addicted to the vice of licentiousness, his slaves had little opportunity for relaxation from wearying labor, were supplied with the scantiest means of sustaining their toil by necessary food, and had no security for personal rights. The natural tendency of slavery is to convert the master into a tyrant, and the slave into the cringing, treacherous, false, and thieving victim of tyranny. Riley and his slaves were no exception to the general rule, but might be cited as apt illustrations of the nature of the relation.

CHAPTER THREE

My Boyhood and Youth

Early employment • Slave-life • Food, lodging, clothing
• Amusements • Gleams of sunshine • My knight-errantry
• Become an overseer and general superintendent

MY EARLIEST EMPLOYMENTS WERE, TO CARRY BUCKETS OF WATER TO THE men at work, and to hold a horse-plough, used for weeding between the rows of corn. As I grew older and taller, I was entrusted with the care of master's saddle-horse. Then a hoe was put into my hands, and I was soon required to do the day's work of a man; and it was not long before I could do it, at least as well as my associates in misery.

The everyday life of a slave on one of our southern plantations, however frequently it may have been described, is generally little understood at the north; and must be mentioned as a necessary illustration of the character and habits of the slave and the slaveholder, created and perpetuated by their relative position. The principal food of those upon my master's plantation consisted of cornmeal, and salt herrings; to which was added in summer a little buttermilk, and the few vegetables which each might raise for himself and his family, on the little piece of ground which was assigned to him for the purpose, called a truck patch.

In ordinary times we had two regular meals in a day: breakfast at twelve o'clock, after laboring from daylight, and supper when the work of the remainder of the day was over. In harvest season we had three. Our dress was of tow-cloth; for the children nothing but a shirt;

for the older ones a pair of pantaloons or a gown in addition, according to the sex. Besides these, in the winter a round jacket or overcoat, a wool hat once in two or three years, for the males, and a pair of coarse shoes once a year.

We lodged in log huts, and on the bare ground. Wooden floors were an unknown luxury. In a single room were huddled, like cattle, ten or a dozen persons, men, women and children. All ideas of refinement and decency were, of course, out of the question. There were neither bedsteads, nor furniture of any description. Our beds were collections of straw and old rags, thrown down in the corners and boxed in with boards; a single blanket the only covering. Our favorite way of sleeping, however, was on a plank, our heads raised on an old jacket and our feet toasting before the smouldering fire. The wind whistled and the rain and snow blew in through the cracks, and the damp earth soaked in the moisture till the floor was miry as a pigsty. Such were our houses. In these wretched hovels were we penned at night, and fed by day; here were the children born and the sick—neglected.

Notwithstanding this system of management I grew to be a robust and vigorous lad. At fifteen years of age there were few who could compete with me in work or sport. I was as lively as a young buck, and running over with animal spirits. I could run faster, wrestle better, and jump higher than anybody about me, and at an evening shakedown in our own or a neighbor's kitchen, my feet became absolutely invisible from the rate at which they moved. All this caused my master and my fellow slaves to look upon me as a wonderfully smart fellow, and prophecy the great things I should do when I became a man. My vanity became vastly inflamed, and I fully coincided in their opinion. Julius Caesar never aspired and plotted for the imperial crown more ambitiously than did I to out-hoe, out-reap, out-husk, out-dance, out-everything every competitor; and from all I can learn he never enjoyed his triumph half as much. One word of commendation from the petty despot who ruled over us would set me up for a month.

I have no desire to represent the life of slavery as an experience of nothing but misery. God be praised, that however hedged in by circumstances, the joyful exuberance of youth will bound at times over them all. Ours is a light-hearted race. The sternest and most covetous master cannot frighten or whip the fun out of us; certainly old Riley never did out of me. In those days I had many a merry time, and would have had, had I lived with nothing but moccasins and rattlesnakes in Okafenoke swamp. Slavery did its best to make me wretched; I feel no particular obligation to it; but nature, or the blessed God of youth and joy, was mightier than slavery. Along with memories of miry cabins, frosted feet, weary toil under the blazing sun, curses and blows, there flock in others, of jolly Christmas times, dances before old massa's door for the first drink of eggnog, extra meat at holiday times, midnight visits to apple orchards, broiling stray chickens, and first-rate tricks to dodge work. The God who makes the pup gambol, and the kitten play, and the bird sing, and the fish leap, was the author in me of many a light-hearted hour. True it was, indeed, that the fun and freedom of Christmas, at which time my master relaxed his front, was generally followed up by a portentous back-action, under which he drove and cursed worse than ever; still the fun and freedom were fixed facts; we had had them and he could not help it.

Besides these pleasant memories I have others of a deeper and richer kind. I early learned to employ my spirit of adventure for the benefit of my fellow-sufferers. The condition of the male slave is bad enough; but that of the female, compelled to perform unfit labor, sick, suffering, and bearing the peculiar burdens of her own sex unpitied and unaided, as well as the toils which belong to the other, is one that must arouse the spirit of sympathy in every heart not dead to all feeling. The miseries which I saw many of the women suffer often oppressed me with a load of sorrow. No *white* knight, rescuing white fair ones from cruel oppression, ever felt the throbbing of a chivalrous heart more intensely than I, a *black* knight, did, in running down a chicken in an out-of-the way place to hide till dark, and then carry to some poor overworked black fair one, to whom it was at once food, luxury, and medicine. No Scotch borderer, levying black mail or sweeping off a drove of cattle, ever felt more assured of the justice of his act than I of mine, in driving a mile or two into the woods a pig or a sheep, and slaughtering it for the good of those whom Riley was starving. I felt good, moral, heroic. The beautiful combination of a high time and a benevolent act—the harmonious interplay of nature and grace—was absolutely entrancing. I felt then the excellency of a sentiment I have since found expressed in a hymn:

> Religion never was designed
> To make our pleasures less.

Was this wrong? I can only say in reply, that, at this distance of time, my conscience does not reproach me for it. Then I esteemed it among the best of my deeds. It was my training in the luxury of doing good, in the divinity of a sympathetic heart, in the righteousness of indignation against the cruel and oppressive. There and then was my soul made conscious of its heavenly original. This, too, was all the chivalry of which my circumstances and condition in life admitted. I love the sentiment in its splendid environment of castles, and tilts, and gallantry; but having fallen on other times, I love it also in the homely guise of Sambo as Paladin, Dinah as outraged maiden, and old Riley as grim oppressor.

By means of the influence thus acquired, the increased amount of work thus done upon the farm, and by the detection of the knavery of the overseer, who plundered his employer for more selfish ends, and through my watchfulness was caught in the act and dismissed, I was promoted to be superintendent of the farm work, and managed to raise more than double the crops, with more cheerful and willing labor, than was ever seen on the estate before.

Yes, I was now practically overseer. My pride and ambition had made me master of every kind of farm work. But like all ambition its reward was increase of burdens. The crops of wheat, oats, barley, potatoes, corn, tobacco, all had to be cared for by me. I was often compelled to start at midnight with the wagon for the distant market, to drive on through mud and rain till morning, sell the produce, reach home hungry and tired, and nine times out of ten reap my sole reward in curses for not getting higher prices. My master was a fearful blasphemer. Clearly as he saw my profitableness to him, he was too much of a brute, and too great a fool through his brutality, to reward me with kindness or even decent treatment. Previous to my attaining this important station, however, an incident occurred which produced so powerful an influence on my intellectual development, my prospect of improvement in character, as well as condition, my chance of religious culture, and in short, on my whole nature, body and soul, that it deserves especial notice and commemoration. This, however, requires another chapter.

> CHAPTER FOUR <

MY CONVERSION

A good man • Hear a sermon for the first time • Its effect upon
me • Prayer and communion • Its first fruits

MY HEART EXULTS WITH GRATITUDE WHEN I MENTION THE NAME OF
a good man who first taught me the blessedness of religion. His name
was John McKenny. He lived at Georgetown, a few miles only from
Riley's plantation; his business was that of a baker, and his character
was that of an upright, benevolent Christian. He was noted especially
for his detestation of slavery, and his resolute avoidance of the employment of slave labor in his business. He would not even hire a slave, the
price of whose toil must be paid to his master, but contented himself
with the work of his own hands, and with such free labor as he could
procure. His reputation was high, not only for this almost singular
abstinence from what no one about him thought wrong, but for his
general probity and excellence. This man occasionally served as a
minister of the Gospel, and preached in a neighborhood where
preachers were somewhat rare at that period. One Sunday when he
was to officiate in this way, at a place three or four miles distant, my
mother urged me to ask master's permission to go and hear him. I had
so often been beaten for making such a request that I refused to make
it. She still persisted, telling me that I could never become a Christian
if I minded beatings—that I must take up my cross and bear it. She was
so grieved at my refusal that she wept. To gratify her I concluded to
try the experiment, and accordingly went to my master and asked

permission to attend the meeting. Although such permission was not given freely or often, yet his favor to me was shown for this once by allowing me to go, without much scolding, but not without a pretty distinct intimation of what would befall me if I did not return immediately after the close of the service. I hurried off, pleased with the opportunity, but without any definite expectations of benefit or amusement; for up to this period of my life, and I was then eighteen years old, I had never heard a sermon, nor any discourse or conversation whatever, upon religious topics, except what I had heard from my mother, on the responsibility of all to a Supreme Being. When I arrived at the place of meeting, the services were so far advanced that the speaker was just beginning his discourse, from the text, Hebrews ii. 9: "That he, by the grace of God, should taste of death for every man." This was the first text of the Bible to which I had ever listened, knowing it to be such. I have never forgotten it, and scarcely a day has passed since, in which I have not recalled it, and the sermon that was preached from it.

The divine character of Jesus Christ, his tender love for mankind, his forgiving spirit, his compassion for the outcast and despised, his cruel crucifixion and glorious ascension, were all depicted, and some of the points were dwelt on with great power; great, at least, to me, who then heard of these things for the first time in my life. Again and again did the preacher reiterate the words "*for every man.*" These glad tidings, this salvation, were not for the benefit of a select few only. They were for the slave as well as the master, the poor as well as the rich, for the persecuted, the distressed, the heavy-laden, the captive; for me among the rest, a poor, despised, abused creature, deemed of others fit for nothing but unrequited toil—but mental and bodily degradation. O, the blessedness and sweetness of feeling that I was LOVED! I would have died that moment, with joy, for the compassionate Saviour about whom I was hearing. "He loves me," "he looks down in compassion from heaven on me," "he died to save my soul," "he'll welcome me to the skies," I kept repeating to myself. I was transported with delicious joy. I seemed to see a glorious being, in a cloud of splendor, smiling down from on high. In sharp contrast with the experience of the contempt and brutality of my earthly master, I basked in the sunshine of the benignity of this divine being. "He'll be my dear refuge—he'll wipe away all tears from my eyes." "Now I can bear all things; nothing will seem hard after this." I felt sorry that "Massa Riley" didn't know him, sorry he should live such a coarse, wicked, cruel life. Swallowed up in the beauty of the divine love, I loved my enemies, and prayed for them that did despitefully use and entreat me.

Revolving the things which I had heard in my mind as I went home, I became so excited that I turned aside from the road into the woods, and prayed to God for light and for aid with an earnestness, which, however unenlightened, was at least sincere and heartfelt; and which the subsequent course of my life has led me to imagine was acceptable to Him who heareth prayer. At all events, I date my conversion, and my awakening to a new life—a consciousness of power and a destiny superior to anything I had before conceived of—from this day, so memorable to me. I used every means and opportunity of inquiry into religious matters; and so deep was my conviction of their superior importance to everything else, so clear my perception of my own faults, and so undoubting my observation of the darkness and sin that surrounded me, that I could not help talking much on these subjects with those about me; and it was not long before I began to pray with them, and exhort them, and to impart to the poor slaves those little glimmerings of light from another world, which had reached my own eye. In a few years I became quite an esteemed preacher among them, and I will not believe it is vanity which leads me to think I was useful to some.

I must return, however, for the present, to the course of my life in secular affairs, the facts of which it is my principal object to relate.

CHAPTER FIVE

MAIMED FOR LIFE

Taking care of my drunken master • His fight with an overseer
• Rescue him • Am terribly beaten by the overseer • My master
seeks redress at law, but fails • Sufferings then and since
• Retain my post as superintendent

THE DIFFERENCE BETWEEN THE MANNER IN WHICH IT WAS DESIGNED
that all men should regard one another as children of the same.
Father, and the manner in which men actually do treat each other, as
if they were placed here for mutual annoyance and destruction, is
well exemplified by an incident that happened to me within a year or
two from this period; that is, when I was nineteen or twenty years old.
My master's habits were such as were common enough among the
dissipated planters of the neighborhood; and one of their frequent
practices was to assemble on Saturday or Sunday, which were their
holidays, and gamble, run horses, or fight game-cocks, discuss politics,
and drink whiskey and brandy and water all day long. Perfectly aware
that they would not be able to find their own way home at night, each
one ordered his body-servant to come after him and help him home.
I was chosen for this confidential duty by my master; and many is the
time I have held him on his horse, when he could not hold himself in
the saddle, and walked by his side in darkness and mud from the tavern to his house. Of course, quarrels and brawls of the most violent
description were frequent consequences of these meetings; and whenever they became especially dangerous, and glasses were thrown, dirks

drawn, and pistols fired, it was the duty of the slaves to rush in, and each one drag his master from the fight, and carry him home. To tell the truth, this was a part of my business for which I felt no reluctance. I was young, remarkably athletic and self-relying, and in such affrays I carried it with a high hand, and would elbow my way among the whites—whom it would have been almost death for me to strike—seize my master and drag him out, mount him on his horse, or crowd him into his buggy, with the ease with which I would handle a bag of corn. I knew that I was doing for him what he could not do for himself, and showing my superiority to others, and acquiring their respect in some degree, at the same time.

On one of these occasions my master got into a quarrel with his brother's overseer, Bryce Litton. All present sided with Litton against him, and soon there was a general row. I was sitting, at the time, out on the front steps of the tavern, and, hearing the scuffle, rushed in to look after my charge. My master, a stout man and a terrible bruiser, could generally hold his own in an ordinary general fight, and clear a handsome space around him; but now he was cornered, and a dozen were striking at him with fists, crockery, chairs, and anything that came handy. The moment he saw me he hallooed, "That's it, Sie! Pitch in! Show me fair play." It was a rough business, and I went in roughly, shoving, tripping, and doing my best for the rescue. With infinite trouble, and many a bruise on my own head and shoulders, I at length got him out of the room. He was crazy with drink and rage, and struggled hard with me to get back and renew the fight. But I managed to force him into his wagon, jump in, and drive off.

By ill-luck, in the height of the scuffle, Bryce Litton got a severe fall. Whether the whisky he had drank, or a chance shove from me, was the cause, I am unable to say. He, however, attributed it to me, and treasured up his vengeance for the first favorable opportunity. The opportunity soon came.

About a week afterwards I was sent by my master to a place a few miles distant, on horseback, with some letters. I took a short cut through a lane, separated by gates from the high road, and bounded by a fence on each side. This lane passed through some of the farm owned by my master's brother, and his overseer was in the adjoining field, with three negroes, when I went by. On my return, half an hour afterwards, the overseer was sitting on the fence; but I could see nothing of the black fellows. I rode on, utterly unsuspicious of any trouble; but as I approached he jumped off the fence, and at the same moment two of the negroes sprang up from under the bushes where they had been concealed, and stood with him immediately in front of me, while the third sprang over the fence just behind me. I was thus enclosed between what I could no longer doubt were hostile forces. The overseer seized my horse's bridle, and ordered me to alight, in the usual elegant phraseology addressed by such men to slaves. I asked what I was to alight for. "To take the cursedest flogging you ever had in your life, you d—d black scoundrel." "But what am I to be flogged for, Mr. L.?" I asked. "Not a word," said he, "but 'light at once, and take off your jacket." I saw there was nothing else to be done, and slipped off the horse on the opposite side from him. "Now take off your shirt," cried he; and as I demurred at this, he lifted a stick he had in his hand to strike me, but so suddenly and violently that he frightened the horse, which broke away from him and ran home. I was thus left without means of escape, to sustain the attacks of four men, as well as I might. In avoiding Mr. L.'s blow, I had accidentally got into a corner of the fence, where I could not be approached except in front. The overseer called upon the negroes to seize me; but they, knowing something of my physical power, were rather slow to obey. At length they did their best, and as they brought themselves within my reach, I knocked them down successively; and one of them trying to trip up my feet when he was down, I gave him a kick with my heavy shoe, which knocked out several teeth, and sent him howling away.

Meanwhile Bryce Litton played away on my head with a stick, not heavy enough, indeed, to knock me down, but drawing blood freely; shouting all the while, "Won't you give up! Won't you give up! You black son of a bitch!" Exasperated at my defence, he suddenly seized a heavy fence-rail, and rushed at me to bring matters to a sudden close. The ponderous blow fell; I lifted my arm to ward it off; the bone cracked like a pipe-stem, and I fell headlong to the ground. Repeated blows then rained on my back, till both shoulder-blades were broken, and the blood gushed copiously from my mouth. In vain the negroes interposed. "Didn't you see the damned nigger strike me?" Of course they must say "yes," although the lying coward had avoided close quarters, and fought with his stick alone. At length, his vengeance satisfied, he desisted, telling me to learn what it was to strike a white man. Meanwhile an alarm had been raised at the house by the return of the horse without his rider, and my master started off with a small party to learn what the trouble was. When he first saw me he was swearing with rage. "You've been fighting, you damned nigger!" I told him Bryce Litton had been beating me, because I shoved him the other night at the tavern, when they had a fuss. Seeing how much I was injured, he became still more fearfully mad; and after having me carried home, mounted his horse and rode over to Montgomery Court House, to enter a complaint. Little good came of it. Litton swore that when he spoke to me in the lane, I "sassed" him, jumped off my horse and made at him, and would have killed him but for the help of his negroes. Of course no negro's testimony could be admitted against a white man, and he was acquitted. My master was obliged to pay all the costs of court; and although he had the satisfaction of calling Litton a liar and scoundrel, and giving him a tremendous bruising, still even this partial compensation was rendered less gratifying by what followed, which was a suit for damages and a heavy fine.

My sufferings after this cruel treatment were intense. Besides my broken arm and the wounds on my head, I could feel and hear the pieces of my shoulder-blades grate against each other with every breath. No physician or surgeon was called to dress my wounds; and I never knew one to be called on Riley's estate on any occasion whatever. "A nigger will get well anyway," was a fixed principle of faith, and facts seemed to justify it. The robust, physical health produced by a life of outdoor labor, made our wounds heal up with as little inflammation as they do in the case of cattle. I was attended by my master's sister, Miss Patty, as we called her, the Esculapius of the plantation. She was a powerful, big-boned woman, who flinched at no responsibility, from wrenching out teeth to setting bones. I have seen her go into the house and get a rifle to shoot a furious ox that the negroes were in vain trying to butcher. She splintered my arm and bound up my back as well as she knew how. Alas! It was but cobbler's work. From that day to this I have been unable to raise my hands as high as my head. It was five months before I could work at all, and the first time I tried to plough, a hard knock of the colter against a stone shattered my shoulder-blades again, and gave me even greater agony than at first. And so I have gone through life maimed and mutilated. Practice in time enabled me to perform many of the farm labors with considerable efficiency; but the free, vigorous play of muscle and arm was gone forever.

My situation as overseer I retained, together with the especial favor of my master, who was not displeased either with saving the expense of a large salary for a white superintendent, or with the superior crops I was able to raise for him. I will not deny that I used his property more freely than he would have done himself, in supplying his people with better food; but if I cheated him in this way, in small matters, it was unequivocally for his own benefit in more important ones; and I accounted, with the strictest honesty, for every dollar I received in the sale of the property entrusted to me. Gradually the disposal of everything raised on the farm—the wheat, oats, hay, fruit, butter, and whatever else there might be—was confided to me, as it was quite evident that I could and did sell for better prices than anyone else he could employ; and he was quite incompetent to attend to the business himself. For many years I was his factotum, and supplied him with all his means for all his purposes, whether they were good or bad. I had no reason to think highly of his moral character; but it was my duty to be faithful to him in the position in which he placed me; and I can boldly declare, before God and man, that I was so. I forgave him the causeless blows and injuries he had inflicted on me in childhood and youth, and was proud of the favor he now showed me, and of the character and reputation I had earned by strenuous and persevering efforts.

CHAPTER SIX

A RESPONSIBLE JOURNEY

My marriage • Marriage of my master • His ruin • Comes to me
for aid • A great enterprise undertaken • Long and successful
journey • Incidents by the way • Struggle between inclination
and duty • Duty triumphant

WHEN I WAS ABOUT TWENTY-TWO YEARS OF AGE, I MARRIED A VERY
efficient, and, for a slave, a very well-taught girl, belonging to a neighboring family, reputed to be pious and kind, whom I first met at the
religious meetings which I attended. She has borne me twelve children, eight of whom still survive and promise to be the comfort of my
declining years.

Things remained in this condition for a considerable period; my
occupations being to superintend the farming operations, and to sell
the produce in the neighboring markets of Washington and Georgetown. Many respectable people, yet living there, may possibly have
some recollection of "Siah," or "Sie," (as they used to call me), as their
market-man; but if they have forgotten me, I remember them with an
honest satisfaction.

After passing his youth in the manner I have mentioned in a general way, and which I do not wish more particularly to describe, my
master, at the age of forty-five, or upwards, married a young woman of
eighteen, who had some little property, and more thrift. Her economy
was remarkable, and was certainly no addition to the comfort of the
establishment. She had a younger brother, Francis, to whom Riley was

21

appointed guardian, and who used to complain—not without reason, I am confident—of the meanness of the provision made for the household; and he would often come to me, with tears in his eyes, to tell me he could not get enough to eat. I made him my friend for life, by sympathising in his emotions and satisfying his appetite, sharing with him the food I took care to provide for my own family. He is still living, and, I understand, one of the wealthiest men in Washington city.

After a time, however, continual dissipation was more than a match for domestic saving. My master fell into difficulty, and from difficulty into a lawsuit with a brother-in-law, who charged him with dishonesty in the management of property confided to him in trust. The lawsuit was protracted enough to cause his ruin of itself.

Harsh and tyrannical as my master had been, I really pitied him in his present distress. At times he was dreadfully dejected, at others crazy with drink and rage. Day after day would he ride over to Montgomery Court House about his business, and every day his affairs grew more desperate. He would come into my cabin to tell me how things were going, but spent the time chiefly in lamenting his misfortunes and cursing his brother-in-law. I tried to comfort him as best I could. He had confidence in my fidelity and judgment, and partly through pride, partly through that divine spirit of love I had learned to worship in Jesus, I entered with interest into all his perplexities. The poor, drinking, furious, moaning creature was utterly incapable of managing his affairs. Shiftlessness, licentiousness and drink had complicated them as much as actual dishonesty.

One night in the month of January, long after I had fallen asleep, he came into my cabin and waked me up. I thought it strange, but for a time he said nothing and sat moodily warming himself at the fire. Then he began to groan and wring his hands. "Sick, massa?" said I. He made no reply but kept on moaning. "Can't I help you anyway, massa?" I spoke tenderly, for my heart was full of compassion at his wretched appearance. At last, collecting himself, he cried, "Oh, Sie! I'm ruined, ruined, ruined!" "How so, massa?" "They've got judgment against me, and in less than two weeks every nigger I've got will be put up and sold." Then he burst into a storm of curses at his brother-in-law. I sat silent, powerless to utter a word. Pity for him and terror at the anticipation of my own family's future fate filled my heart. "And now, Sie," he continued, "there's only one way I can save anything. You can do it; won't you, won't you?" In his distress he rose and actually threw his arms around me. Misery had levelled all distinctions. "If I can do it, massa, I will. What is it?" Without replying he went on, "won't you, won't you? I raised you, Sie; I made you overseer; I know I've abused you, Sie, but I didn't mean it." Still he avoided telling me what he wanted. "Promise me you'll do it, boy." He seemed resolutely bent on having my promise first, well knowing from past experience that what I agreed to do I spared no pains to accomplish. Solicited in this way, with urgency and tears, by the man whom I had so zealously served for over thirty years, and who now seemed absolutely dependent upon his slave—impelled, too, by the fear which he skilfully awakened, that the sheriff would seize everyone who belonged to him, and that all would be separated, or perhaps sold to go to Georgia, or Louisiana—an object of perpetual dread to the slave of the more northern States—I consented, and promised faithfully to do all I could to save him from the fate impending over him.

At last the proposition came. "I want you to run away, Sie, to your master Amos in Kentucky, and take all the servants along with you." I could not have been more startled had he asked me to go to the moon. Master Amos was his brother. "Kentucky, massa? Kentucky? I don't know the way." "O, it's easy enough for a smart fellow like you to find it; I'll give you a pass and tell you just what to do." Perceiving that I hesitated, he endeavored to frighten me by again referring to the terrors of being sold to Georgia.

For two or three hours he continued to urge the undertaking, appealing to my pride, my sympathies, and my fears, and at last, appalling as it seemed, I told him I would do my best. There were eighteen negroes, besides my wife, two children and myself, to transport nearly a thousand miles, through a country about which I knew nothing, and in mid-winter—for it was the month of February, 1825. My master proposed to follow me in a few months, and establish himself in Kentucky.

My mind once made up, I set earnestly about the needful preparations. They were few and easily made. A one-horse wagon, well stocked with oats, meal, bacon, for our own and the horse's support, was soon made ready. My pride was aroused in view of the importance of my responsibility, and heart and soul I became identified with my master's project of running off his negroes. The second night after the scheme was formed we were under way. Fortunately for the success of the undertaking, these people had long been under my direction, and were devotedly attached to me in return for the many alleviations I had afforded to their miserable condition, the comforts I had procured them, and the consideration I had always manifested for them. Under these circumstances no difficulty arose from want of submission to my authority. The dread of being separated, and sold away down south, should they remain on the old estate, united them as one man, and kept them patient and alert.

We started from home about eleven o'clock at night, and till the following noon made no permanent halt. The men trudged on foot, the children were put into the wagon, and now and then my wife rode for a while. On we went through Alexandria, Culpepper, Fauquier, Harper's Ferry, Cumberland, over the mountains on the National Turnpike, to Wheeling. In all the taverns along the road were regular places for the droves of negroes continually passing along under the system of the internal slave trade. In these we lodged, and our lodging constituted our only expense, for our food we carried with us. To all who asked questions I showed my master's pass, authorizing me to conduct his negroes to Kentucky, and often was the encomium of "smart nigger" bestowed on me, to my immense gratification.

At the places where we stopped for the night, we often met negro-drivers with their droves, who were almost uniformly kept chained to prevent them from running away. The inquiry was often propounded to me by the drivers, "Whose niggers are those?" On being informed, the next inquiry usually was, "Where are they going?" "To Kentucky." "Who drives them?" "Well, I have charge of them," was my reply. "What a smart nigger!" was the usual exclamation, with an oath. "Will your master sell you? Come in and stop with us." In this way I was often invited to pass the evening with them in the barroom; their negroes, in the meantime, lying chained in the pen, while mine were scattered around at liberty.

Arriving at Wheeling, in pursuance of the plan laid down by my master, I sold the horse and wagon, and purchased a large boat, called in that region a yawl. Our mode of locomotion was now decidedly more agreeable than tramping along day after day, at the rate we had kept up ever since leaving home. Very little labor at the oars was necessary. The tide floated us steadily along, and we had ample leisure to sleep and recruit our strength.

A new and unexpected trouble now assailed me. On passing along the Ohio shore, we were repeatedly told by persons conversing with us, that we were no longer slaves, but free men, if we chose to be so. At Cincinnati, especially, crowds of colored people gathered round us, and insisted on our remaining with them. They told us we were fools to think of going on and surrendering ourselves up to a new owner; that now we could be our own masters, and put ourselves out of all reach of pursuit. I saw the people under me were getting much excited. Divided counsels and signs of insubordination began to manifest themselves. I began, too, to feel my own resolution giving way. Freedom had ever been an object of my ambition, though no other means of obtaining it had occurred to me but purchasing myself. I had never dreamed of running away. I had a sentiment of honor on the subject. The duties of the slave to his master as appointed over him in the Lord, I had ever heard urged by ministers and religious men. It seemed like outright stealing. And now I felt the devil was getting the upper hand of me. Strange as all this may seem, I really felt it then. Entrancing as the idea was, that the coast was clear for a run for freedom, that I might liberate my companions, might carry off my wife and children, and some day own a house and land, and be no longer despised and abused—still my notions of right were against it. I had promised my master to take his property to Kentucky, and deposit it with his brother Amos. Pride, too, came in to confirm me. I had undertaken a great thing; my vanity had been flattered all along the road by hearing myself praised; I thought it would be a feather in my cap to carry it through thoroughly; and had often painted the scene in my imagination of the final surrender of my charge to master Amos, and the immense admiration and respect with which he would regard me.

Under the influence of these impressions, and seeing that the allurements of the crowd were producing a manifest effect, I sternly assumed the captain, and ordered the boat to be pushed off into the stream. A shower of curses followed me from the shore; but the negroes under me, accustomed to obey, and, alas! Too degraded and ignorant of the advantages of liberty to know what they were forfeiting, offered no resistance to my command.

Often since that day has my soul been pierced with bitter anguish at the thought of having been thus instrumental in consigning to the infernal bondage of slavery so many of my fellow-beings. I have wrestled in prayer with God for forgiveness. Having experienced myself the sweetness of liberty, and knowing too well the after misery of numbers of many of them, my infatuation has seemed to me the unpardonable sin. But I console myself with the thought that I acted according to my best light, though the light that was in me was darkness. Those were my days of ignorance. I knew not the glory of free manhood. I knew not that the title-deed of the slave-owner is robbery and outrage.

What advantages I may have personally lost by thus throwing away an opportunity of obtaining freedom, I know not; but the perception of my own strength of character, the feeling of integrity, the sentiment of high honor, I thus gained by obedience to what I believed right, these advantages I do know and prize. He that is faithful over a little, will alone be faithful over much. Before God, I tried to do my best, and the error of judgment lies at the door of the degrading system under which I had been nurtured.

CHAPTER SEVEN

A NEW HOME

Become a Methodist preacher • My poor companions sold
• My agony • Sent for again • Interview with a kind Methodist
preacher • Visit free soil and begin my struggle for freedom

I ARRIVED AT DAVIS COUNTY, KENTUCKY, ABOUT THE MIDDLE OF APRIL, 1825, and delivered myself and my companions to Mr. Amos Riley, the brother of my owner, who had a large plantation, with from eighty to one hundred negroes. His house was situated about five miles south of the Ohio River, and fifteen miles above the Yellow Banks, on Big Blackfords Creek. There I remained three years, expecting my master to follow, and was employed meantime on the farm, of which I had the general management, in consequence of the recommendation for ability and honesty which I brought with me from Maryland. The situation was, in many respects, more comfortable than that I had left. The farm was larger and more fertile, and there was a greater abundance of food, which is, of course, one of the principal sources of the comfort of a slave, debarred as he is from so many enjoyments which other men can obtain. Sufficiency of food is a pretty important item in any man's account of life; but is tenfold more so in that of the slave, whose appetite is always stimulated by as much labor as he can perform, and whose mind is little occupied by thought on subjects of deeper interest. My post of superintendent gave me some advantages, too, of which I did not fail to avail myself; particularly with regard to those religious privileges, which, since I first heard of Christ and

Christianity, had greatly occupied my mind. In Kentucky the opportunities of attending on the preaching of whites, as well as of blacks, were more numerous; and partly by attending them, and the camp-meetings which occurred from time to time, and partly from studying carefully my own heart, and observing the developments of character around me, in all the stations of life which I could watch, I became better acquainted with those religious feelings which are deeply implanted in the breast of every human being, and learned by practice how best to arouse them, and keep them excited, how to stir up the callous and indifferent, and, in general, to produce some good religious impressions on the ignorant and thoughtless community by which I was surrounded.

No great amount of theological knowledge is requisite for the purpose. If it had been, it is manifest enough that preaching never could have been my vocation; but I am persuaded that, speaking from the fulness of a heart deeply impressed with its own sinfulness and imperfection, and with the mercy of God, in Christ Jesus, my humble ministrations have not been entirely useless to those who have had less opportunity than myself to reflect upon these all important subjects. It is certain that I could not refrain from the endeavor to do what I saw others doing in this field; and I labored at once to improve myself and those about me in the cultivation of the harvests which ripen only in eternity. I cannot but derive some satisfaction, too, from the proofs I have had that my services have been acceptable to those to whom they have been rendered. In the course of three years, from 1825 to 1828, I availed myself of all the opportunities of improvement which occurred, and was admitted as a preacher by a Quarterly Conference of the Methodist Episcopal Church.

In the spring of the year 1828, news arrived from my master that he was unable to induce his wife to accompany him to Kentucky, and that he must therefore remain where he was. He sent out an agent to sell all his slaves, except me and my family, and to carry back the proceeds to him. And now another of those heartrending scenes was to be witnessed, which had impressed itself so deeply on my childish soul. Husbands and wives, parents and children, were to be separated forever. Affections, which are as strong in the African as in the European, were to be cruelly disregarded; and the iron selfishness generated by the hateful "institution," was to be exhibited in its most odious and naked deformity. I was exempted from a personal share in the dreadful calamity; but I could not see, without the deepest grief, the agony which I recollected in my own mother, and which was again brought before my eyes in the persons with whom I had been long associated; nor could I refrain from the bitterest feeling of hatred of the system, and those who sustain it. What else, indeed, can be the feeling of the slave, liable at every moment of his life to these frightful and unnecessary calamities, which may be caused by the caprice of the abandoned, or the supposed necessities of the better part of the slaveholders, and inflicted upon him without sympathy or redress, under the sanction of the laws which uphold the institution?

As I surveyed this scene, and listened to the groans and outcries of my afflicted companions, the torments of hell seized upon me. My eyes were opened, and the guilty madness of my conduct in preventing them from availing themselves of the opportunity for acquiring freedom, which offered itself at Cincinnati, overwhelmed me. This, then, was the reward and end of all my faithfulness to my master. I had thought of him only and his interests, not of them or their welfare. Oh! What would I not have given to have had the chance offered once more! And now, through me, were they doomed to wear out life miserably in the hot and pestilential climate of the far south. Death would have been welcome to me in my agony. From that hour I saw through, hated, and cursed the whole system of slavery. One absorbing purpose occupied my soul—freedom, self-assertion, deliverance from the cruel caprices and fortunes of dissolute tyrants. Once to get away, with my wife and children, to some spot where I could feel that they were indeed *mine*—where no grasping master could stand between me and them, as arbiter of their destiny—was a heaven yearned after with insatiable longing. For it I stood ready to pray, toil, dissemble, plot like a fox, and fight like a tiger. All the noble instincts of my soul, and all the ferocious passions of my animal nature, were aroused and quickened into vigorous action.

The object of my old master Riley in directing that I and my family should be exempted from the sale, was a desire on his part to get me back to Maryland, and employ me in his own service. His best farms had been taken away from him, and but a few tracts of poor land remained. After his slaves had been run off, he cultivated these with hired labor, and month by month grew poorer and more desperate. He had written to his brother Amos to give me a pass and let me travel back; but this his brother was reluctant to do, as I saved him the expense of an overseer, and he moreover knew that no legal steps could be taken to force him to comply. I knew of all this, but dared not seem anxious to return, for fear of exciting suspicion.

In the course of the summer of 1828, a Methodist preacher, a most excellent white man, visited our neighborhood, and I became acquainted with him. He was soon interested in me, and visited me frequently, and one day talked to me in a confidential manner about my position. He said I ought to be free; that I had too much capacity to be confined to the limited and comparatively useless sphere of a slave; "and though," said he, "I must not be known to have spoken to you on this subject, yet if you will obtain Mr. Amos' consent to go to see your old master in Maryland, I will try and put you in a way by which I think you may succeed in buying yourself." He said this to me more than once; and as it was in harmony with all my aspirations and wishes, was flattering to my self-esteem, and gratified my impatience to bring matters to a direct issue, I now resolved to make the attempt to get the necessary leave. The autumn work was over, I was no longer needed in the fields, and a better chance would never offer itself. Still I dreaded to make the proposal. So much hung on it, such fond hopes were bound up with it, that I trembled for the result.

I opened the subject one Sunday morning while shaving Mr. Amos, and adroitly managed, by bringing the shaving brush close into his mouth whenever he was disposed to interrupt me, to "get a good say" first. Of course I made no allusion to my plan of buying myself; but urged my request on the sole ground of a desire to see my old master. To my surprise he made little objection. I had been faithful to him, and gained, in his rude way of showing it, his regard. Long before spring I would be back again. He even told me I had earned such a privilege.

The certificate he gave me allowed me to pass and repass between Kentucky and Maryland as servant of Amos Riley. Furnished with this, and with a letter of recommendation from my Methodist friend to a brother preacher in Cincinnati, I started about the middle of September, 1828, for the east.

A new era in my history now opened upon me. A letter I carried with me to a kind-hearted man in Cincinnati procured me a number of invaluable friends, who entered heart and soul into my plans. They procured me an opportunity to preach in two or three of the pulpits of the city, and I made my appeal with that eloquence which spontaneously breaks forth from a breast all alive and fanned into a glow by an inspiring project. Contact with those who were free themselves, and a proud sense of exultation in taking my destiny into my own hands, gave me the sacred "gift of tongues." I was pleading an issue of life and death, of heaven and hell, and such as heard me felt this in their hearts. In three or four days I left the city with no less a sum than one hundred and sixty dollars in my pockets, and with a soul jubilant with thanksgiving, and high in hope, directed my steps towards Chillicothe, to attend the session of the Ohio Conference of the Methodist Episcopal Church. My kind friend accompanied me, and by his influence and exertions still further success attended me.

By his advice I then purchased a decent suit of clothes and an excellent horse, and travelled from town to town preaching as I went. Everywhere I met with kindness. The contrast between the respect with which I was treated and the ordinary abuse, or at best insolent familiarity, of plantation life, gratified me in the extreme, as it must anyone who has within him one spark of personal dignity as a man. The sweet enjoyment of sympathy, moreover, and the hearty "God speed you, brother!" which accompanied every dollar I received, were to my long starved heart a celestial repast, and angels' food. Liberty was a glorious hope in my mind; not as an escape from toil, for I rejoiced in toil when my heart was in it, but as the avenue to a sense of self-respect, to ennobling occupation, and to association with superior minds. Still, dear as was the thought of liberty, I still clung to my determination to gain it in one way only—by purchase. The cup of my affliction was not yet full enough to lead me to disregard all terms with my master.

CHAPTER EIGHT

RETURN TO MARYLAND

Reception from my old master • A slave again • Appeal to an old
friend • Buy my freedom • Cheated and betrayed • Back to Kentucky,
and a slave again

BEFORE I LEFT OHIO AND SET MY FACE TOWARDS MONTGOMERY
County, I was master of two hundred and seventy-five dollars, besides
my horse and clothes. Proud of my success, I enjoyed the thought of
showing myself once more in the place where I had been known simply as "Riley's head nigger"; and it was with no little satisfaction that
about Christmas I rode up to the old house.

My master gave me a boisterous reception, and expressed great
delight at seeing me. "Why, what in the devil have you been doing,
Sie? You've turned into a regular black gentleman." My horse and
dress sorely puzzled him, and I soon saw it began to irritate him. The
clothes I wore were certainly better than his. And already the workings
of that tyrannical hate with which the coarse and brutal, who have no
inherent superiority, ever regard the least sign of equality in their
dependents, were visible in his manner. His face seemed to say, "I'll
take the gentleman out of you pretty soon." I gave him such an
account of my preaching as, while it was consistent with the truth, and
explained my appearance, did not betray to him my principal purpose. He soon asked to see my pass, and when he found it authorized
me to return to Kentucky, handed it to his wife, and desired her to put
it into his desk. The manœuvre was cool and startling. I heard the old

prison gate clang, and the bolt shoot into the socket once more. But I said nothing, and resolved to manœuvre also.

After putting my horse in the stable I retired to the kitchen, where my master told me I was to sleep for the night. O, how different from my accommodations in the free States, for the last three months, was the crowded room, with its dirt floor, and filth, and stench! I looked around me with a sensation of disgust. The negroes present were strangers to me, being slaves that Mrs. Riley had brought to her husband. "Fool that I was to come back!" I found my mother had died during my absence, and every tie which had ever connected me with the place was broken. The idea of lying down with my nice clothes in this nasty sty was insufferable. Full of gloomy reflections at my loneliness, and the poverty-stricken aspect of the whole farm, I sat down; and while my companions were snoring in unconsciousness, I kept awake, thinking how I should escape from the accursed spot. I knew of but one friend to whom I could appeal—"Master Frank," the brother of Riley's wife, before mentioned, who was now of age, and had established himself in business in Washington. I knew he would take an interest in me, for I had done much to lighten his sorrows when he was an abused and harshly treated boy in the house. To him I resolved to go, and as soon as I thought it time to start, I saddled my horse and rode up to the house. It was early in the morning, and my master had already gone to the tavern on his usual business, when Mrs. Riley came out to look at my horse and equipments. "Where are you going, 'Siah?" was the natural question. I replied, "I am going to Washington, mistress, to see Mr. Frank, and I must take my pass with me, if you please." "O, everybody knows you here; you won't need your pass." "But I can't go to Washington without it. I may be met by some surly stranger, who will stop me and plague me, if he can't do anything worse." "Well, I'll get it for you," she answered; and glad was I to see her return with it in her hand, and to have her give it to me, while she little imagined its importance to my plan.

My reception by Master Frank was all I expected, as kind and hearty as possible. He was delighted at my appearance, and I immediately told him all my plans and hopes. He entered cordially into them, and expressed, as he felt, I doubt not, a strong sympathy for me. I found that he thoroughly detested Riley, whom he charged with having defrauded him of a large proportion of his property which he had held as guardian, though, as he was not at warfare with him, he readily agreed to negotiate for my freedom, and bring him to the most favorable terms. Accordingly, in a few days he rode over to the house, and had a long conversation with him on the subject of my emancipation. He disclosed to him the facts that I had got some money, and *my pass,* and urged that I was a smart fellow, who was bent upon getting his freedom, and had served the family faithfully for many years; that I had really paid for myself a hundred times over, in the increased amount of produce I had raised by my skill and influence; and that if he did not take care, and accept a fair offer when I made it to him, he would find someday that I had the means to do without his help, and that he would see neither me nor my money; that with my horse and my pass I was pretty independent of him already, and he had better make up his mind to do what was really inevitable, and do it with a good grace. By such arguments as these, Mr. Frank not only induced him to think of the thing, but before long brought him to an actual bargain, by which he agreed to give me my manumission papers for four hundred and fifty dollars, of which three hundred and fifty dollars were to be in cash, and the remainder in my note. My money and my horse enabled me to pay the cash at once, and thus my great hope seemed in a fair way of being realized.

Some time was spent in the negotiation of this affair, and it was not until the ninth of March, 1829, that I received my manumission papers in due form of law. I prepared to start at once on my return to Kentucky; and on the tenth, as I was getting ready, in the morning, for my journey, my master accosted me in the most friendly manner, and entered into conversation with me about my plans. He asked me what I was going to do with my certificate of freedom; whether I was going to show it if questioned on the road. I told him, "Yes." "You'll be a fool if you do," he rejoined. "Some slave-trader will get hold of it and tear it up, and the first thing you know, you'll be thrown into prison, sold for your jail fees, and be in his possession before any of your friends can help you. Don't show it at all. Your pass is enough. Let me enclose your papers for you under cover to my brother. Nobody will dare to break a seal, for that is a state-prison matter; and when you arrive in Kentucky you will have it with you all safe and sound."

For this friendly advice, as I thought it, I felt extremely grateful. Secure in my happiness, I cherished no suspicion of others. I accordingly permitted him to enclose my precious papers in an envelope composed of several wrappers, and after he had sealed it with three seals, and directed it to his brother in Davies county, Kentucky, in my care, I carefully stowed it in my carpet bag. Leaving immediately for Wheeling, to which place I was obliged to travel on foot, I there took boat, and in due time reached my destination. I was arrested repeatedly on the way; but by insisting always on being carried before a magistrate, I succeeded in escaping all serious impediments by means of my pass, which was quite regular, and could not be set aside by any responsible authority.

The boat which took me down from Louisville, landed me about dark, and my walk of five miles brought me to the plantation at bedtime. I went directly to my own cabin, and found my wife and little ones well. Of course we had enough to communicate to each other. I soon found that I had something to learn as well as to tell. Letters had reached the "great house"—as the master's was always called—long before I arrived, telling them what I had been doing. The children of the family had eagerly communicated the good news to my wife—how I had been preaching, and raising money, and making a bargain for my freedom. It was not long before Charlotte began to question me, with much excitement, about how I raised the money. She evidently thought I had stolen it. Her opinion of my powers as a preacher was not exalted enough to permit her to believe I had gained it as I really did. It was the old story of the prophet without honor in his own place. I contrived however to quiet her fears on this score. "But how are you going to raise enough to pay the remainder of the thousand dollars?" "What thousand dollars?" "The thousand dollars you were to give for your freedom." O, how those words smote me! At once I suspected treachery. Again and again I questioned her as to what she had heard. She persisted in repeating the same story as the substance of my master's letters. Master Amos said I had paid three hundred and fifty dollars down, and when I had made up six hundred and fifty more I was to have my free papers. I now began to perceive the trick that had been played upon me, and to see the management by which Riley had contrived that the only evidence of my freedom should be kept from every eye but that of his brother Amos, who was requested to retain it until I had made up the balance I was reported to have agreed to pay. Indignation is a faint word to express my deep sense of such villainy. I was alternately beside myself with rage, and paralyzed with despair. My dream of bliss was over. What could I do to set myself right? The only witness to the truth, Master Frank, was a thousand miles away. I could neither write to him, or get anyone else to write. Every man about me who could write was a slaveholder. I dared not go before a magistrate with my papers, for fear I should be seized and sold down the river before anything could be done. I felt that every man's hand would be against me. "My God! My God! Why hast them forsaken me?" was my bitter cry. One thing only seemed clear. My papers must never be surrendered to Master Amos. I told my wife I had not seen them since I left Louisville. They might be in my bag, or they might be lost. At all events I did not wish to look myself. If she found them there, and hid them away, out of my knowledge, it would be the best disposition to make of them.

The next morning, at the blowing of the horn, I went out to find Master Amos. I found him sitting on a stile, and as I drew near enough for him to recognize me, he shouted out a hearty welcome in his usual chaste style. "Why, halloa, Sie! Is that you? Got back, eh! Why, you old son of a bitch, I'm glad to see you! Drot your blood, drot your blood, why, you're a regular black gentleman!" And he surveyed my dress with an appreciative grin. "Well, boy, how's your master? Isaac says you want to be free. Want to be free, eh! I think your master treats you pretty hard, though. Six hundred and fifty dollars don't come so easy in old Kentuck. How does he ever expect you to raise all that. It's too much, boy, it's too much." In the conversation that followed I found my wife was right. Riley had no idea of letting me off, and supposed I could contrive to raise six hundred and fifty as easily as one hundred dollars.

Master Amos soon asked me if I had not a paper for him. I told him I had had one, but the last I saw of it was at Louisville, and now it was not in my bag, and I did not know what had become of it. He sent me back to the landing to see if it had been dropped on the way. Of course I did not find it. He made, however, little stir about it, for he had intentions of his own to keep me working for him, and regarded the whole as a trick of his brother's to get money out of me. All he said about the loss was, "Well, boy, bad luck happens to everybody, sometimes."

All this was very smooth and pleasant to a man who was in a frenzy of grief at the base and apparently irremediable trick that had been played upon him. I had supposed that I should now be free to start out and gain the other hundred dollars which would discharge my obligation to my master. But I soon saw that I was to begin again with my old labors. It was useless to give expression to my feelings, and I went about my work with as quiet a mind as I could, resolved to trust in God, and never despair.

CHAPTER NINE

Taken South, Away from Wife and Children

Start for New Orleans • Study navigation on the Mississippi
• The captain struck blind • Find some of my old
companions • The lower depths

Things went on in this way about a year. From time to time Master Amos joked me about the six hundred and fifty dollars, and said his brother kept writing to know why I did not send something. It was "diamond cut diamond" with the two brothers. Mr. Amos had no desire to play into the hands of Mr. Isaac. He was glad enough to secure my services to take care of his stock and his people.

One day my master suddenly informed me that his son Amos, a young man about twenty-one years of age, was going down the river to New Orleans, with a flat-boat loaded with produce, and that I was to go with him. He was to start the next day, and I was to accompany him and help him dispose of his cargo to the best advantage.

This intimation was enough. Though it was not distinctly stated, yet I well knew what was intended, and my heart sunk within me at the near prospect of this fatal blight to all my long-cherished hopes. There was no alternative but death itself; and I thought that there was hope as long as there was life, and I would not despair even yet. The expectation of my fate, however, produced the degree of misery nearest to that of despair; and it is in vain for me to attempt to describe the wretchedness I experienced as I made ready to go on board the flat-boat. I had little preparation to make, to be sure; and there was but one thing that seemed to me important. I asked my wife to sew up my manumission paper securely in a piece of cloth, and to sew that again round my person. I thought that having possession of it might be the means of saving me yet, and I would not neglect anything that offered the smallest chance of escape from the frightful servitude that threatened me.

The immediate cause of this movement on the part of Master Amos I never fully understood. It grew out of a frequent exchange of letters, which had been kept up between him and his brother in Maryland. Whether as a compromise between their rival claims it was agreed to sell me and divide the proceeds, or that Master Amos, in fear of my running away, had resolved to turn me into riches without wings, for his own profit, I never knew. The fact of his intention, however, was clear enough; and God knows it was a fearful blow.

My wife and children accompanied me to the landing, where I bade them an adieu which might be for life, and then stepped into the boat, which I found manned by three white men, who had been hired for the trip. Mr. Amos and myself were the only other persons on board. The load consisted of beef-cattle, pigs, poultry, corn, whisky, and other articles from the farm, and from some of the neighboring estates, which were to be sold as we dropped down the river, wherever they could be disposed of to the greatest advantage. It was a common trading voyage to New Orleans, in which I was embarked, the interest of which consisted not in the incidents that occurred, not in storms, or shipwreck, or external disaster of any sort; but in the storm of passions contending within me, and the imminent risk of the shipwreck of my soul, which was impending over me nearly the whole period of the voyage. One circumstance, only, I will mention, illustrating, as other events in my life have often done, the counsel of the Saviour, "He that will be chief among you, let him be your servant."

We were, of course, all bound to take our trick at the helm in turn, sometimes under direction of the captain, and sometimes on our own responsibility, as he could not be always awake. In the daytime there was less difficulty than at night, when it required someone who knew the river, to avoid sandbars and snags, and the captain was the only person on board who had this knowledge. But whether by day or by night, as I was the only negro in the boat, I was made to stand at least three tricks (white men are very fond of such tricks) to any other person's one; so that, from being much with the captain, and frequently thrown upon my own exertions, I learned the art of steering and managing the boat far better than the rest. I watched the manœuvres necessary to shoot by a sawyer, to land on a bank, or avoid a snag, or a steamboat, in the rapid current of the Mississippi, till I could do it as well as the captain. After a while he was attacked by a disease of the eyes; they became very much inflamed and swollen. He was soon rendered totally blind, and unable to perform his share of duty. This disorder is not an unfrequent consequence of exposure to the light of the sun, doubled in intensity as it is by the reflection from the river. I was the person who could best take his place, and I was in fact master of the boat from that time till our arrival at New Orleans.

After the captain became blind we were obliged to lie by at night, as none of the rest of us had been down the river before; and it was necessary to keep watch all night, to prevent depredations by the negroes on shore, who used frequently to attack such boats as ours, for the sake of the provisions on board.

On our way down the river we stopped at Vicksburg, and I got permission to visit a plantation a few miles from the town, where some of my old companions whom I had brought from Kentucky were living. It was the saddest visit I ever made. Four years in an unhealthy climate and under a hard master had done the ordinary work of twenty. Their cheeks were literally caved in with starvation and disease, and their bodies infested with vermin. No hell could equal the misery they described as their daily portion. Toiling half naked in malarious marshes, under a burning, maddening sun, and poisoned by swarms of musquitoes and black gnats, they looked forward to death as their only deliverance. Some of them fairly cried at seeing me there, and at thought of the fate which they felt awaited me. Their worst fears of being sold down South had been more than realized. I went away sick at heart, and to this day the sight of that wretched group haunts me.

CHAPTER TEN

A TERRIBLE TEMPTATION

Sigh for death • A murder in my heart • The axe raised
• Conscience speaks and I am saved • God be praised!

NOW ALL OUTWARD NATURE SEEMED TO FEED MY GLOOMY THOUGHTS.
I know not what most men see in voyaging down the Mississippi. If
gay and hopeful, probably much of beauty and interest. If eager
merchants, probably a golden river, freighted with the wealth of
nations. I saw nothing but portents of woe and despair. Wretched
slave-pens; a smell of stagnant waters; half-putrid carcasses of horses
or oxen floating along, covered with turkey buzzards and swarms of
green flies—these are the images with which memory crowds my
mind. My faith in God utterly gave way. I could no longer pray or trust.
He had abandoned me and cast me off forever. I looked not to him
for help. I saw only the foul miasmas, the emaciated frames of my
negro companions; and in them saw the sure, swift, loving interven-
tion of the one unfailing friend of the wretched—death! Yes; death
and the grave! "There the wicked cease from troubling, and the weary
are at rest. There the prisoners rest together; they hear not the voice of
the oppressor." Two years of this would kill me. I dwelt on the thought
with melancholy yet sweet satisfaction. Two years! And then I should
be free. Free! Ever my cherished hope, though not as I had thought
it would come.

As I paced backwards and forwards on the deck, during my watch,
it may well be believed I revolved in my mind many a painful and

passionate thought. After all that I had done for Isaac and Amos Riley, after all the regard they had professed for me, such a return as this for my services, such an evidence of their utter disregard of my claims upon them, and the intense selfishness with which they were ready to sacrifice me, at any moment, to their supposed interest, turned my blood to gall, and changed me from a lively, and, I will say, a pleasant-tempered fellow, into a savage, morose, dangerous slave. I was going not at all as a lamb to the slaughter; but I felt myself becoming more ferocious every day; and as we approached the place where this iniquity was to be consummated, I became more and more agitated with an almost uncontrollable fury. I said to myself, "If this is to be my lot, I cannot survive it long. I am not so young as those whose wretched condition I have but just now seen, and if it has brought them to such a condition, it will soon kill me. I am to be taken by my masters and owners, who ought to be my grateful friends, to a place and a condition where my life is to be shortened, as well as made more wretched. Why should I not prevent this wrong if I can, by shortening their lives, or those of their agents, in accomplishing such detestable injustice? I can do the last easily enough. They have no suspicion of me, and they are at this moment under my control, and in my power. There are many ways in which I can dispatch them and escape; and I feel that I should be justified in availing myself of the first good opportunity." These were not thoughts which just flitted across my mind's eye and then disappeared. They fashioned themselves into shapes which grew larger and seemed firmer every time they presented themselves; and at length my mind was made up to convert the phantom shadow into a positive reality.

I resolved to kill my four companions, take what money there was in the boat, then to scuttle the craft, and escape to the north. It was a poor plan, maybe, and would very likely have failed; but it was as well contrived, under the circumstances, as the plans of murderers usually are; and blinded by passion, and stung to madness as I was, I could not see any difficulty about it. One dark, rainy night, within a few days' sail of New Orleans, my hour seemed to have come. I was alone on the deck; Master Amos and the hands were all asleep below, and I crept down noiselessly, got hold of an axe, entered the cabin, and looking by the aid of the dim light there for my victims, my eye fell upon Master Amos, who was nearest to me; my hand slid along the axe-handle; I raised it to strike the fatal blow—when suddenly the thought came to me, "What! Commit *murder!* And you a Christian?" I had not called it murder before. It was self-defence—it was preventing others from murdering me—it was justifiable, it was even praiseworthy. But now, all at once, the truth burst upon me that it was a crime. I was going to kill a young man who had done nothing to injure me, but was only obeying commands which he could not resist; I was about to lose the fruit of all my efforts at self-improvement, the character I had acquired, and the peace of mind that had never deserted me. All this came upon me instantly, and with a distinctness which almost made me think I heard it whispered in my ear; and I believe I even turned my head to listen. I shrunk back, laid down the axe, and thanked God, as I have done every day since, that I had not committed murder.

My feelings were still agitated, but they were changed. I was filled with shame and remorse for the design I had entertained, and with the fear that my companions would detect it in my face, or that a careless word would betray my guilty thoughts. I remained on deck all night, instead of rousing one of the men to relieve; and nothing brought composure to my mind but the solemn resolution I then made, to resign myself to the will of God, and take with thankfulness, if I could, but with submission, at all events, whatever he might decide should be my lot. I reflected that if my life were reduced to a brief term, I should have less to suffer; and that it was better to die with a Christian's hope, and a quiet conscience, than to live with the incessant recollection of a crime that would destroy the value of life, and under the weight of a secret that would crush out the satisfaction that might be expected from freedom and every other blessing.

It was long before I recovered my self-control and serenity; but I believe that no one but those to whom I have told the story myself, ever suspected me of having entertained such thoughts for a moment.

CHAPTER ELEVEN

PROVIDENTIAL DELIVERANCE

Offered for sale • Examined by purchasers • Plead with my young
master in vain • Man's extremity, God's opportunity • Good for evil
• Return North • My increased value • Resolve to be a slave no longer

IN A FEW DAYS AFTER THIS TRYING CRISIS IN MY LIFE, WE ARRIVED AT
New Orleans. The little that remained of our cargo was soon sold, the
men were discharged, and nothing was left but to dispose of me, and
break up the boat, and then Master Amos would take passage on a
steamboat, and go home. There was no longer any disguise about the
disposition which was to be made of me. Master Amos acknowledged
that such were his instructions, and he set about fulfilling them. Several planters came to the boat to look at me; I was sent on some hasty
errand that they might see how I could run; my points were canvassed
as those of a horse would have been; and, doubtless, some account of
my various faculties entered into the discussion of the bargain, that my
value as a domestic animal might be enhanced. Master Amos had
talked, with apparent kindness, about getting me a good master, who
would employ me as a coachman, or as a house-servant; but as time
passed on I could discern no particular effort of the kind.

In our intervals of leisure I tried every possible means to move his
heart. With tears and groans I besought him not to sell me away from
my wife and children. I dwelt on my past services to his father, and
called to his remembrance a thousand things I had done for him personally. I told him about the wretched condition of the slaves I had

seen near Vicksburg. Sometimes he would shed tears himself, and say he was sorry for me. But still I saw his purpose was unchanged. He now kept out of my way as much as possible, and forestalled every effort I made to talk with him. His conscience evidently troubled him. He knew he was doing a cruel and wicked thing, and wanted to escape from thinking about it. I followed him up hard, for I was supplicating for my life. I fell down and clung to his knees in entreaties. Sometimes when too closely pressed, he would curse and strike me. May God forgive him. And yet it was not all his fault. He was made so by the accursed relation of slave-master and slave. I was property—not a man, not a father, not a husband. And the laws of property and self-interest, not of humanity and love, bore sway.

At length everything was wound up but this single affair. I was to be sold the next day, and Master Amos was to set off on his return, in a steamboat, at six o'clock in the afternoon. I could not sleep that night; its hours seemed interminably long, though it was one of the shortest of the year. The slow way in which we had come down had brought us to the long days and heats of June; and everybody knows what the climate of New Orleans is at that period of the year.

And now occurred one of those sudden, marked interpositions of Providence, by which in a moment the whole current of a human being's life is changed; one of those slight and, at first, unappreciated contingencies, by which the faith that man's extremity is God's opportunity is kept alive. Little did I think, when a little before daylight Master Amos called me and told me he felt sick, how much my future was bound up in those few words. His stomach was disordered, and I advised him to lie down again, thinking it would soon pass off. Before long he felt worse, and it was soon evident that the river fever was upon him. He became rapidly ill, and by eight o'clock in the morning was utterly prostrate. The tables were now turned. I was no longer property, no longer a brute beast to be bought and sold, but his only friend in the midst of strangers. Oh, how different was his tone from what it had been the day before! He was now the supplicant. A poor, terrified object, afraid of death, and writhing with pain, there lay the late arbiter of my destiny. How he besought me to forgive him. "Stick to me, Sie! Stick to me, Sie! Don't leave me, don't leave me. I'm sorry

I was going to sell you." Sometimes he would say he had only been joking, and never intended to part with me. Yes, the tables were utterly turned. He entreated me to dispatch matters, sell the flat-boat in which we had been living, and get him and his trunk, containing the proceeds of the trip, on board the steamer as quick as possible. I attended to all his requests, and by twelve o'clock that day he was in one of the cabins of the steamer appropriated to sick passengers.

O, my God! How my heart sang jubilees of praise to Thee, as the steamboat swung loose from the levee and breasted the mighty tide of the Mississippi! Away from this land of bondage and death! Away from misery and despair! Once more exulting hope possessed me. This time if I do not open my way to freedom, may God never give me chance again!

Before we had proceeded many hours on our voyage, a change for the better appeared in my young master. The change of air in a measure revived him; and well it was for him that such was the case. Short as his illness had been, the fever had raged like a fire, and he was already near death. I watched and nursed him like a mother; for all remembrance of personal wrong was obliterated at sight of his peril. His eyes followed me in entreaty wherever I went. His strength was so entirely gone that he could neither speak nor move a limb, and could only indicate his wish for a teaspoonful of gruel, or something to moisten his throat, by a feeble motion of his lips. I nursed him carefully and constantly. Nothing else could have saved his life. It hung by a thread for a long time. We were as much as twelve days in reaching home, for the water was low at that season, particularly in the Ohio river; and when we arrived at our landing he was still unable to speak, and could only be moved on a sheet or a litter. Something of this sort was soon fixed up at the landing, on which he could be carried to the house, which was five miles off; and I got a party of the slaves belonging to the estate to form relays for the purpose. As we approached the house, the surprise at seeing me back again, and the perplexity to imagine what I was bringing along, with such a party, were extreme; but the discovery was soon made which explained the strange appearance; and the grief of father and mother, and brothers and sisters, made itself seen and heard. Loud and long were the lamentations over poor Amos; and when the family came a little to themselves, great were the commendations bestowed upon me for my care of him and of the property.

Although we reached home by the tenth of July, it was not until the middle of August that Master Amos was well enough to leave his chamber. To do him justice, he manifested strong gratitude towards me. Almost his first words after recovering his strength sufficiently to talk, were in commendation of my conduct. "If I had sold him I should have died." On the rest of the family no permanent impression seemed to have been made. The first few words of praise were all I ever received. I was set at my old work. My merits, whatever they were, instead of exciting sympathy or any feeling of attachment to me, seemed only to enhance my market value in their eyes. I saw that my master's only thought was to render me profitable to himself. From him I had nothing to hope, and I turned my thoughts to myself and my own energies.

Before long I felt assured another attempt would be made to dispose of me. Providence seemed to have interfered once to defeat the scheme, but I could not expect such extraordinary circumstances to be repeated; and I was bound to do everything in my power to secure myself and my family from the wicked conspiracy of Isaac and Amos Riley against my life, as well as against my natural rights, and those which I had acquired, under even the barbarous laws of slavery, by the money I had paid for myself. If Isaac would only have been honest enough to adhere to his bargain, I would have adhered to mine, and paid him all I had promised. But his attempt to kidnap me again, after having pocketed three-fourths of my market value, in my opinion absolved me from all obligation to pay him any more, or to continue in a position which exposed me to his machinations.

CHAPTER TWELVE

ESCAPE FROM BONDAGE

Solitary musings • Preparations for flight • A long good night to master • A dark night on the river • Night journeys in Indiana • On the brink of starvation • A kind woman • A new style of drinking cup • Reach Cincinnati

DURING THE BRIGHT AND HOPEFUL DAYS I SPENT IN OHIO, WHILE AWAY on my preaching tour, I had heard much of the course pursued by fugitives from slavery, and became acquainted with a number of benevolent men engaged in helping them on their way. Canada was often spoken of as the only sure refuge from pursuit, and that blessed land was now the desire of my longing heart. Infinite toils and perils lay between me and that haven of promise; enough to daunt the stoutest heart; but the fire behind me was too hot and fierce to let me pause to consider them. I knew the North Star—blessed be God for setting it in the heavens! Like the Star of Bethlehem, it announced where my salvation lay. Could I follow it through forest, and stream, and field, it would guide my feet in the way of hope. I thought of it as my God-given guide to the land of promise far away beneath its light. I knew that it had led thousands of my poor, hunted brethren to freedom and blessedness. I felt energy enough in my own breast to contend with privation and danger; and had I been a free, untrammeled man, knowing no tie of father or husband, and concerned for my own safety only, I would have felt all difficulties light in view of the hope that was set before me. But, alas! I had a wife and four dear children; how should I provide for them? Abandon them I could not; no! Not even for the blessed boon of freedom. They, too, must go. They, too, must share with me the life of liberty.

It was not without long thought upon the subject that I devised a plan of escape. But at last I matured it. My mind fully made up, I communicated the intention to my wife. She was overwhelmed with terror. With a woman's instinct she clung to hearth and home. She knew nothing of the wide world beyond, and her imagination peopled it with unseen horrors. We should die in the wilderness—we should be hunted down with bloodhounds—we should be brought back and whipped to death. With tears and supplications she besought me to remain at home, contented. In vain I explained to her our liability to be torn asunder at any moment; the horrors of the slavery I had lately seen; the happiness we should enjoy together in a land of freedom, safe from all pursuing harm. She had not suffered the bitterness of my lot, nor felt the same longing for deliverance. She was a poor, ignorant, unreasoning slave-woman.

I argued the matter with her at various times, till I was satisfied that argument alone would not prevail. I then told her deliberately, that though it would be a cruel trial for me to part with her, I would nevertheless do it, and take all the children with me except the youngest, rather than remain at home, only to be forcibly torn from her, and sent down to linger out a wretched existence in the hell I had lately visited. Again she wept and entreated, but I was sternly resolute. The whole night long she fruitlessly urged me to relent; exhausted and maddened, I left her, in the morning, to go to my work for the day. Before I had gone far, I heard her voice calling me, and waiting till I came up, she said, at last, she would go with me. Blessed relief! My tears of joy flowed faster than had hers of grief.

Our cabin, at this time, was near the landing. The plantation itself extended the whole five miles from the house to the river. There were several distinct farms, all of which I was over-seeing, and therefore I was riding about from one to another every day. Our oldest boy was at the house with Master Amos; the rest of the children were with my wife.

The chief practical difficulty that had weighed upon my mind, was connected with the youngest two of the children. They were of three and two years, respectively, and of course would have to be carried. Both stout and healthy, they were a heavy burden, and my wife had declared that I should break down under it before I had got five miles from home. Sometime previously I had directed her to make me a large knapsack of tow cloth, large enough to hold them both, and arranged with strong straps to go round my shoulders. This done, I had practised carrying them night after night, both to test my own strength and accustom them to submit to it. To them it was fine fun, and to my great joy I found I could manage them successfully. My wife's consent was given on Thursday morning, and I resolved to start on the night of the following Saturday. Sunday was a holiday; on Monday and Tuesday I was to be away on farms distant from the house; thus several days would elapse before I should be missed, and by that time I should have got a good start.

At length the eventful night arrived. All things were ready, with the single exception that I had not yet obtained my master's permission for little Tom to visit his mother. About sundown I went up to the great house to report my work, and after talking for a time, started off, as usual, for home; when, suddenly appearing to recollect something I had forgotten, I turned carelessly back, and said, "O, Master Amos, I most forgot. Tom's mother wants to know if you won't let him come down a few days; she wants to mend his clothes and fix him up a little." "Yes, boy, yes; he can go." "Thankee, Master Amos; good night, good night. The Lord bless you!" In spite of myself I threw a good deal of emphasis into my farewell. I could not refrain from an inward chuckle at the thought—how long a good night that will be! The coast was all clear now, and, as I trudged along home, I took an affectionate look at the well-known objects on my way. Strange to say, sorrow mingled with my joy; but no man can live anywhere long without feeling some attachment to the soil on which he labors.

It was about the middle of September, and by nine o'clock all was ready. It was a dark, moonless night, when we got into the little skiff, in which I had induced a fellow slave to set us across the river. It was an anxious moment. We sat still as death. In the middle of the stream the good fellow said to me, "It will be the end of me if this is ever found out; but you won't be brought back alive, Sie, will you?" "Not if

I can help it," I replied; and I thought of the pistols and knife I had bought sometime before of a poor white. "And if they're too many for you, and you get seized, you'll never tell my part in this business?" "Not if I'm shot through like a sieve." "That's all," said he, "and God help you." Heaven reward him. He, too, has since followed in my steps; and many a time in a land of freedom have we talked over that dark night on the river.

In due time we landed on the Indiana shore. A hearty, grateful farewell, such as none but companions in danger can know, and I heard the oars of the skiff propelling him home. There I stood in the darkness, my dear ones with me, and the all unknown future before us. But there was little time for reflection. Before daylight should come on, we must put as many miles behind us as possible, and be safely hidden in the woods. We had no friends to look to for assistance, for the population in that section of the country was then bitterly hostile to the fugitive. If discovered, we should be seized and lodged in jail. In God was our only hope. Fervently did I pray to him as we trudged on cautiously and steadily, and as fast as the darkness and the feebleness of my wife and boys would allow. To her, indeed, I was compelled to talk sternly; she trembled like a leaf, and even then implored me to return.

For a fortnight we pressed steadily on, keeping to the road during the night, hiding whenever a chance vehicle or horseman was heard, and during the day burying ourselves in the woods. Our provisions were rapidly giving out. Two days before reaching Cincinnati they were utterly exhausted. All night long the children cried with hunger, and my poor wife loaded me with reproaches for bringing them into such misery. It was a bitter thing to hear them cry, and God knows I needed encouragement myself. My limbs were weary, and my back and shoulders raw with the burden I carried. A fearful dread of detection ever pursued me, and I would start out of my sleep in terror, my heart beating against my ribs, expecting to find the dogs and slave-hunters after me. Had I been alone I would have borne starvation, even to exhaustion, before I would have ventured in sight of a house in quest of food. But now something must be done; it was necessary to run the risk of exposure by daylight upon the road.

The only way to proceed was to adopt a bold course. Accordingly, I left our hiding place, took to the road, and turned towards the south, to lull any suspicion that might be aroused were I to be seen going the other way. Before long I came to a house. A furious dog rushed out at me, and his master following to quiet him, I asked if he would sell me a little bread and meat. He was a surly fellow. "No, he had nothing for niggers!" At the next I succeeded no better, at first. The man of the house met me in the same style; but his wife, hearing our conversation, said to her husband, "How can you treat any human being so? If a dog was hungry I would give him something to eat." She then added, "We have children, and who knows but they may someday need the help of a friend." The man laughed, and told her that she might take care of niggers, he wouldn't. She asked me to come in, loaded a plate with venison and bread, and, when I laid it into my handkerchief, and put a quarter of a dollar on the table, she quietly took it up and put it in my handkerchief, with an additional quantity of venison. I felt the hot tears roll down my cheeks as she said "God bless you"; and I hurried away to bless my starving wife and little ones.

A little while after eating the venison, which was quite salt, the children become very thirsty, and groaned and sighed so that I went off stealthily, breaking the bushes to keep ray path, to find water. I found a little rill, and drank a large draught. Then I tried to carry some in my hat; but, alas! It leaked. Finally, I took off both shoes, which luckily had no holes in them, rinsed them out, filled them with water, and carried it to my family. They drank it with great delight. I have since then sat at splendidly furnished tables in Canada, the United States, and England; but never did I see any human beings relish anything more than my poor famishing little ones did that refreshing draught out of their father's shoes. That night we made a long run, and two days afterward we reached Cincinnati.

CHAPTER THIRTEEN

JOURNEY TO CANADA

Good Samaritans • Alone in the wilderness • Meet some Indians
• Reach Sandusky • Another friend • All aboard • Buffalo • A "free
nigger" • Frenzy of joy on reaching Canada

I NOW FELT COMPARATIVELY AT HOME. BEFORE ENTERING THE TOWN I
hid my wife and children in the woods, and then walked on alone in
search of my friends. They welcomed me warmly, and just after dusk
my wife and children were brought in, and we found ourselves hospi-
tably cheered and refreshed. Two weeks of exposure to incessant
fatigue, anxiety, rain, and chill, made it indescribably sweet to enjoy
once more the comfort of rest and shelter.

Since I have lived in a land of freedom, I have heard harsh and
bitter words spoken of those devoted men who are banded together
to succor and bid God speed the hunted fugitive; men who, through
pity for the suffering, have voluntarily exposed themselves to hatred,
fines, and imprisonment. If there be a God who will have mercy on the
merciful, great shall be their reward. In the great day when men shall
stand in judgment before the Divine Master, crowds of the outcast and
forsaken of earth shall gather around them, and in joyful tones bear
witness, "We were hungry and ye gave us meat, thirsty and ye gave us
drink, naked and ye clothed us, sick and ye visited us." And he who has
declared that, "inasmuch as ye have done it unto the least of these my
brethren, ye have done it unto me," shall accept the attestation, and
hail them with his welcome, "Come ye blessed of my father." They can

afford to bide their time. Their glory shall yet be proclaimed from the house-tops. Meanwhile may that "peace of God which the world can neither give nor take away" dwell richly in their hearts.

Among such as these—good Samaritans, of whom the Lord would say, "go ye and do likewise"—our lot was now cast. Carefully they provided for our welfare until our strength was recruited, and then they set us thirty miles on our way by wagon.

We followed the same course as before—travelling by night and resting by day—till we arrived at the Scioto, where we had been told we should strike the military road of General Hull, in the last war with Great Britain, and might then safely travel by day. We found the road, accordingly, by the large sycamore and elms which marked its beginning, and entered upon it with fresh spirits early in the day. Nobody had told us that it was cut through the wilderness, and I had neglected to provide any food, thinking we should soon come to some habitation, where we could be supplied. But we travelled on all day without seeing one, and lay down at night, hungry and weary enough. The wolves were howling around us, and though too cowardly to approach, their noise terrified my poor wife and children. Nothing remained to us in the morning but a little piece of dried beef, too little, indeed, to satisfy our cravings, but enough to afflict us with intolerable thirst. I divided most of this among us, and then we started for a second day's tramp in the wilderness. A painful day it was to us. The road was rough, the underbrush tore our clothes and exhausted our strength; trees that had been blown down blocked the way; we were faint with hunger; and no prospect of relief opened up before us. We spoke little, but steadily struggled along; I with my babes on my back, my wife aiding the two other children to climb over the fallen trunks and force themselves through the briers. Suddenly, as I was plodding along a little ahead of my wife and the boys, I heard them call me, and turning round saw my wife prostrate on the ground. "Mother's dying," cried Tom; and when I reached her it seemed really so. From sheer exhaustion she had fallen in surmounting a log. Distracted with anxiety, I feared she was gone. For some minutes no sign of life was manifest; but after a time she opened her eyes, and finally recovering enough to take a few mouthfuls of the beef, her strength returned, and we once more went bravely on our way. I cheered the sad group with hopes I was far from sharing myself. For the first time I was nearly ready to abandon myself to despair. Starvation in the wilderness was the doom that stared me and mine in the face. But again, "man's extremity was God's opportunity."

We had not gone far, and I suppose it was about three o'clock in the afternoon, when we discerned some persons approaching us at no great distance. We were instantly on the alert, as we could hardly expect them to be friends. The advance of a few paces showed me they were Indians, with packs on their shoulders; and they were so near that if they were hostile it would be useless to try to escape. So I walked along boldly, till we came close upon them. They were bent down with their burdens, and had not raised their eyes till now; and when they did so, and saw me coming towards them, they looked at me in a frightened sort of way for a moment, and then, setting up a peculiar howl, turned round, and ran as fast as they could. There were three or four of them, and what they were afraid of I could not imagine, unless they supposed I was the devil, whom they had perhaps heard of as black. But, even then, one would have thought my wife and children might have reässured them. However, there was no doubt they were well frightened, and we heard their wild and prolonged howl, as they ran, for a mile or more. My wife was alarmed, too, and thought they were merely running back to collect more of a party, and then to come and murder us; and she wanted to turn back. I told her they were numerous enough to do that, if they wanted to, without help; and that as for turning back, I had had quite too much of the road behind us, and that it would be a ridiculous thing that both parties should run away. If they were disposed to run, I would follow. We did follow, and the noise soon ceased. As we advanced, we could discover Indians peeping at us from behind the trees, and dodging out of of sight if they thought we were looking at them. Presently we came upon their wigwams, and saw a fine-looking, stately Indian, with his arms folded, waiting for us to approach. He was, apparently, the chief; and, saluting us civilly, he soon discovered we were human beings, and spoke to his young men, who were scattered about, and made them come in and give up their foolish fears. And now curiosity seemed to prevail. Each one wanted to touch the children, who were as shy as partridges with their long life in the woods; and as they shrunk away, and uttered a little cry of alarm, the Indian would jump back too, as if he thought they would bite him. However, a little while sufficed to make them understand what we were, and whither we were going, and what we needed; and as little to set them about supplying our wants, feeding us bountifully, and giving us a comfortable wigwam for our night's rest. The next day we resumed our march, having ascertained from the Indians that we were only about twenty-five miles from the lake. They sent some of their young men to point out the place where we were to turn off, and parted from us with as much kindness as possible.

In passing over the part of Ohio near the lake, where such an extensive plain is found, we came to a spot overflowed by a stream, across which the road passed. I forded it first, with the help of a sounding-pole, and then taking the children on my back, first the two little ones, and then the others, one at a time, and, lastly, my wife, I succeeded in getting them safely across. At this time the skin was worn from my back to an extent almost equal to the size of the knapsack.

One night more was passed in the woods, and in the course of the next forenoon we came out upon the wide plain, without trees, which lies south and west of Sandusky city. The houses of the village were in plain sight. About a mile from the lake I hid my wife and children in the bushes, and pushed forward. I was attracted by a house on the left, between which and a small coasting vessel a number of men were passing and repassing with great activity. Promptly deciding to approach them, I drew near, and scarcely had I come within hailing distance, when the captain of the schooner cried out, "Hollo there, man! You want to work?" "Yes, sir!" shouted I. "Come along, come along; I'll give you a shilling an hour. Must get off with this wind." As I came near, he said, "O, you can't work; you're crippled." "Can't I?" said I; and in a minute I had hold of a bag of corn, and followed the gang in emptying it into the hold. I took my place in the line of laborers next to a colored man, and soon got into conversation with him. "How far is it to Canada?" He gave me a peculiar look, and in a minute I saw he knew all. "Want to go to Canada? Come along with us, then. Our captain's a fine fellow. We're going to Buffalo." "Buffalo; how far is that from

Canada?" "Don't you know, man? Just across the river." I now opened my mind frankly to him, and told him about my wife and children. "I'll speak to the captain," said he. He did so, and in a moment the captain took me aside, and said, "The Doctor says you want to go to Buffalo with your family." "Yes, sir." "Well, why not go with me!" was his frank reply. "Doctor says you've got a family." "Yes sir." "Where do you stop?" "About a mile back." "How long have you been here?" "No time," I answered, after a moment's hesitation. "Come, my good fellow, tell us all about it. You're running away, ain't you?" I saw he was a friend, and opened my heart to him. "How long will it take you to get ready?" "Be here in half an hour, sir." "Well, go along and get them." Off I started; but, before I had run fifty feet, he called me back. "Stop," says he; "you go on getting the grain in. When we get off, I'll lay to over opposite that island, and send a boat back. There's a lot of regular nigger-catchers in the town below, and they might suspect if you brought your party out of the bush by daylight." I worked away with a will. Soon the two or three hundred bushels of corn were aboard, the hatches fastened down, the anchor raised, and the sails hoisted.

I watched the vessel with intense interest as she left her moorings. Away she went before the free breeze. Already she seemed beyond the spot at which the captain agreed to lay to, and still she flew along. My heart sunk within me; so near deliverance, and again to have my hopes blasted, again to be cast on my own resources. I felt that they had been making a mock of my misery. The sun had sunk to rest, and the purple and gold of the west were fading away into grey. Suddenly, however, as I gazed with weary heart, the vessel swung round into the wind, the sails flapped, and she stood motionless. A moment more, and a boat was lowered from her stern, and with steady stroke made for the point at which I stood. I felt that my hour of release had come. On she came, and in ten minutes she rode up handsomely on to the beach.

My black friend and two sailors jumped out, and we started off at once for my wife and children. To my horror, they were gone from the place where I left them. Overpowered with fear, I supposed they had been found and carried off. There was no time to lose, and the men told me I would have to go alone. Just at the point of despair, however, I stumbled on one of the children. My wife, it seemed, alarmed at my long absence, had given up all for lost, and supposed I had fallen into the hands of the enemy. When she heard my voice, mingled with those of the others, she thought my captors were leading me back to make me discover my family, and in the extremity of her terror she had tried to hide herself. I had hard work to satisfy her. Our long habits of concealment and anxiety had rendered her suspicious of everyone; and her agitation was so great that for a time she was incapable of understanding what I said, and went on in a sort of paroxysm of distress and fear. This, however, was soon over, and the kindness of my companions did much to facilitate the matter.

And now we were off for the boat. It required little time to embark our baggage—one convenience, at least, of having nothing. The men bent their backs with a will, and headed steadily for a light hung from the vessel's mast I was praising God in my soul. Three hearty cheers welcomed us as we reached the schooner, and never till my dying day shall I forget the shout of the captain—he was a Scotchman—"Coom up on deck, and clop your wings and craw like a rooster; you're a free nigger as sure as the devil." Round went the vessel, the wind plunged into her sails as though innoculated with the common feeling—the water seethed and hissed passed her sides. Man and nature, and, more than all, I felt the God of man and nature, who breathes love into the heart and maketh the winds his ministers, were with us. My happiness, that night, rose at times to positive pain. Unnerved by so sudden a change from destitution and danger to such kindness and blessed security, I wept like a child.

The next evening we reached Buffalo, but it was to late too cross the river that night. "You see those trees," said the noble hearted captain next morning, pointing to a group in the distance; "they grow on free soil, and as soon as your feet touch that you're a *man*. I want to see you go and be a freeman. I'm poor myself, and have nothing to give you; I only sail the boat for wages; but I'll see you across. Here Green," said he to a ferryman; "what will you take this man and his family for—he's got no money?" "Three shillings." He then took a dollar out of his pocket and gave it to me. Never shall I forget the spirit in which he spoke. He put his hand on my head and said, "Be a good fellow, won't you?" I felt streams of emotion running down in electric courses from head to foot. "Yes," said I; "I'll use my freedom well; I'll give my soul to God." He stood waving his hat as we pushed off for the opposite shore. God bless him! God bless him eternally! Amen!

It was the 28th of October, 1830, in the morning, when my feet first touched the Canada shore. I threw myself on the ground, rolled in the sand, seized handfuls of it and kissed them, and danced round till, in the eyes of several who were present, I passed for a madman. "He's some crazy fellow," said a Colonel Warren, who happened to be there. "O, no, master! Don't you know? I'm free!" He burst into a shout of laughter. "Well, I never knew freedom make a man roll in the sand in such a fashion." Still I could not control myself. I hugged and kissed my wife and children, and, until the first exuberant burst of feeling was over, went on as before.

➔ CHAPTER FOURTEEN ←

New Scenes and a New Home

A poor man in a strange land • Begin to acquire property
• Resume preaching • Boys go to school • What gave me a desire
to learn to read • A day of prayer in the woods

THERE WAS NOT MUCH TIME TO BE LOST, THOUGH IN FROLIC EVEN, AT
this extraordinary moment. I was a stranger in a strange land, and
had to look about me, at once, for refuge and resource. I found a lodging for the night; and the next morning set about exploring the
interior for the means of support. I knew nothing about the country
or the people; but kept my eyes and ears open, and made such inquiries as opportunity afforded. I heard, in the course of the day, of
a Mr. Hibbard, who lived some six or seven miles off, and who was a
rich man, as riches were counted there, with a large farm, and several
small tenements on it, which he was in the habit of letting to his laborers. To him I went, immediately, though the character given him by
his neighbors was not, by any means, unexceptionable good. But I
thought he was not, probably, any worse than those I had been accustomed to serve, and that I could get along with him, if honest and
faithful work would satisfy him. In the afternoon I found him, and soon
struck a bargain with him for employment. I asked him if there was
any house where he would let me live. He said "yes," and led the way
to an old two-story sort of shanty, into the lower story of which the pigs
had broken, and had apparently made it their resting place for some
time. Still, it was a house, and I forthwith expelled the pigs, and set
about cleaning it for the occupancy of a better sort of tenants. With

the aid of hoe and shovel, hot water and a mop, I got the floor into a tolerable condition by midnight, and only then did I rest from my labor. The next day I brought the rest of the Hensons to *my house*, and though there was nothing there but bare walls and floors, we were all in a state of great delight, and my wife laughed and acknowledged that it was worth while, and that it was better than a log cabin with an earth-floor. I begged some straw of Mr. Hibbard, and confining it by logs in the corners of the room, I made beds of it three feet thick, upon which we reposed luxuriously after our long fatigues.

Another trial awaited me which I had not anticipated. In consequence of the great exposures we had been through, my wife and all the children fell sick; and it was not without extreme peril that they escaped with their lives.

My employer soon found that my labor was of more value to him than that of those he was accustomed to hire; and as I consequently gained his favor, and his wife took quite a fancy to mine, we soon procured some of the comforts of life, while the necessaries of food and fuel were abundant. I remained with Mr. Hibbard three years, sometimes working on shares, and sometimes for wages; and I managed in that time to procure some pigs, a cow, and a horse. Thus my condition gradually improved, and I felt that my toils and sacrifices for freedom had not been in vain. Nor were my labors for the improvement of myself and others, in more important things than food and clothing, without effect. It so happened that one of my Maryland friends arrived in this neighborhood, and hearing of my being here, inquired if I ever preached now, and spread the reputation I had acquired elsewhere for my gifts in the pulpit. I had said nothing myself, and had not intended to say anything of my having ever officiated in that way. I went to meeting with others, when I had an opportunity, and enjoyed the quiet of the Sabbath when there was no assembly. I would not refuse to labor in this field, however, when desired to do so; and I hope it is no violation of modesty to state the fact, that I was frequently called upon, not by blacks alone, but by all classes in my vicinity—the comparatively educated, as well as the lamentably ignorant—to speak to them on their duty, responsibility, and immortality, on their obligations to their Maker, their Saviour, and themselves.

It may, nay, I am aware it must, seem strange to many, that a man so ignorant as myself, unable to read, and having heard so little as I had of religion, natural or revealed, should be able to preach acceptably to persons who had enjoyed greater advantages than myself. I can explain it only by reference to our Saviour's comparison of the kingdom of heaven to a plant which may spring from a seed no bigger than a mustard seed, and may yet reach such a size, that the birds of the air may take shelter therein. Religion is not so much knowledge as wisdom; and observation upon what passes without, and reflection upon what passes within a man's heart, will give him a larger growth in grace than is imagined by the devoted adherents of creeds, or the confident followers of Christ, who call him "Lord, Lord," but do not the things which he says.

Mr. Hibbard was good enough to give my eldest boy, Tom, two quarters' schooling, to which the schoolmaster added more, of his own kindness, so that my boy learned to read fluently and well. It was a great advantage, not only to him, but to me; for I used to get him to read much to me in the Bible, especially on Sunday mornings, when I was going to preach; and I could easily commit to memory a few verses, or a chapter, from hearing him read it over.

One beautiful summer Sabbath I rose early, and called him to come and read to me. "Where shall I read, father?" "Anywhere, my son," I answered, for I knew not how to direct him. He opened upon Psalm ciii. "Bless the Lord, O my soul: and all that is within me, bless his holy name"; and as he read this beautiful outpouring of gratitude, which I now first heard, my heart melted within me. I recalled, with all the rapidity of which thought is capable, the whole current of my life; and, as I remembered the dangers and afflictions from which the Lord had delivered me, and compared my present condition with what it had been, not only my heart but my eyes overflowed, and I could neither check nor conceal the emotion which overpowered me. The words, "Bless the Lord, O my soul," with which the Psalm begins and ends, were all I needed, or could use, to express the fullness of my thankful heart. When he had finished, Tom turned to me and asked, "Father, who was David?" He had observed my excitement, and added, "He writes pretty, don't he?" and then repeated his question. It was a question I was utterly unable to answer. I had never heard of David, but could not bear to acknowledge my ignorance to my own child. So I answered evasively, "He was a man of God, my son." "I suppose so," said he, "but I want to know something more about him. Where did he live? What did he do?" As he went on questioning me, I saw it was in vain to attempt to escape, and so I told him frankly I did not know. "Why, father," said he, "can't you read?" This was a worse question than the other, and, if I had any pride in me at the moment, it took it all out of me pretty quick. It was a direct question, and must have a direct answer; so I told him at once I could not. "Why not?" said he. "Because I never had an opportunity to learn, nor anybody to teach me." "Well, you can learn now, father." "No, my son, I am too old, and have not time enough. I must work all day, or you would not have enough to eat." "Then you might do it at night." "But still there is nobody to teach me. I can't afford to pay anybody for it, and, of course, no one can do it for nothing." "Why, father, *I'll teach you*. I can do it, I know. And then you'll know so much more that you can talk better, and preach better." The little fellow was so earnest, there was no resisting him; but it is hard to describe the conflicting feelings within me at such a proposition from such a quarter. I was delighted with the conviction that my children would have advantages I had never enjoyed; but it was no slight mortification to think of being instructed by a child of twelve years old. Yet ambition, and a true desire to learn, for the good it would do my own mind, conquered the shame, and I agreed to try. But I did not reach this state of mind instantly.

I was greatly moved by the conversation I had with Tom, so much so that I could not undertake to preach that day. The congregation were disappointed, and I passed the Sunday in solitary reflection in the woods. I was too much engrossed with the multitude of my thoughts within me to return home to dinner, and spent the whole day in secret meditation and prayer, trying to compose myself, and ascertain my true position. It was not difficult to see that my predicament was one of profound ignorance, and that I ought to use every opportunity of enlightening it. I began to take lessons of Tom, therefore, immediately, and followed it up every evening, by the light of a pine knot, or some hickory bark, which was the only light I could afford. Weeks passed, and my progress was so slow that poor Tom was almost discouraged, and used to drop asleep sometimes, and whine a little over my dullness, and talk to me very much as a schoolmaster talks to a stupid boy, till I began to be afraid that my age, my want of practice in looking at such little scratches, the daily fatigue, and the dim light, would be effectual preventives of my ever acquiring the art of reading. But Tom's perseverance and mine conquered at last, and in the course of the winter I did really learn to read a little.

It was, and has been ever since, a great comfort to me to have made this acquisition; though it has made me comprehend better the terrible abyss of ignorance in which I had been plunged all my previous life. It made me also feel more deeply and bitterly the oppression under which I had toiled and groaned; but the crushing and cruel nature of which I had not appreciated, till I found out, in some slight degree, from what I had been debarred. At the same time it made me more anxious than before to do something for the rescue and the elevation of those who were suffering the same evils I had endured, and who did not know how degraded and ignorant they really were.

CHAPTER FIFTEEN

LIFE IN CANADA

Condition of the blacks in Canada • A tour of exploration
• Appeal to the Legislature • Improvements

AFTER ABOUT THREE YEARS HAD PASSED, I IMPROVED MY CONDITION
again by taking service with a gentleman by the name of Riseley, whose
residence was only a few miles distant, and who was a man of more
elevation of mind than Mr. Hibbard, and of superior abilities. At his
place I began to reflect, more and more, upon the circumstances of
the blacks, who were already somewhat numerous in this region. I was
not the only one who had escaped from the States, and had settled on
the first spot in Canada which they had reached. Several hundreds
of colored persons were in the neighborhood; and, in the first joy of
their deliverance, were going on in a way which, I could see, led to
little or no progress in improvement. They were content to have the
proceeds of their labor at their own command, and had not the ambition for, or the perception of what was within their easy reach, if they
did but know it. They were generally working for hire upon the lands
of others, and had not yet dreamed of becoming independent propri-
etors themselves. It soon became my great object to awaken them to a
sense of the advantages which were within their grasp; and Mr. Riseley,
seeing clearly the justness of my views, and willing to cooperate with
me in the attempt to make them generally known among the blacks,
permitted me to call meetings at his house of those who were known
to be among the most intelligent and successful of our class. At these

meetings we considered and discussed the subject, till we were all of one mind; and it was agreed, among the ten or twelve of us who assembled at them, that we would invest our earnings in land, and undertake the task—which, though no light one certainly would yet soon reward us for our effort—of settling upon wild lands which we could call our own; and where every tree which we felled, and every bushel of corn we raised, would be for ourselves; in other words, where we could secure all the profits of our own labor.

The advantages of this course need not be dwelt upon, in a country which is every day exemplifying it, and has done so for two hundred years and more; and has, by this very means, acquired an indestructible character for energy, enterprise, and self-reliance. It was precisely the Yankee spirit which I wished to instill into my fellow-slaves, if possible; and I was not deterred from the task by the perception of the immense contrast in all the habits and character generated by long ages of freedom and servitude, activity and sloth, independence and subjection. My associates agreed with me, and we resolved to select some spot among the many offered to our choice, where we could colonize, and raise our own crops, eat our own bread, and be, in short, our own masters. I was deputed to explore the country, and find a place to which I would be willing to migrate myself; and they all said they would go with me, whenever such a one should be found. I set out accordingly in the autumn of 1834, and travelled on foot all over the extensive region between lakes Ontario, Erie, and Huron. When I came to the territory east of Lake St. Clair and Detroit River, I was strongly impressed with its fertility, its convenience, and, indeed, its superiority, for our purposes, to any other spot I had seen. I determined this should be the place; and so reported, on my return, to my future companions. They were wisely cautious, however, and sent me off again in the summer, that I might see it at the opposite seasons of the year, and be better able to judge of its advantages. I found no reason to change my opinion, but upon going farther towards the head of Lake Erie, I discovered an extensive tract of government land, which, for some years, had been granted to a Mr. McCormick upon certain conditions, and which he had rented out to settlers upon such terms as he could obtain. This land being already cleared, offered some advantages for the immediate raising of crops, which were not to be overlooked by persons whose resources were so limited as ours; and we determined to go there first, for a time, and with the proceeds of what we could earn there, to make our purchases in Dawn afterwards. This plan was followed, and some dozen or more of us settled upon these lands the following spring, and accumulated something by the crops of wheat and tobacco we were able to raise.

I discovered, before long, that McCormick had not complied with the conditions of his grant, and was not, therefore, entitled to the rent he exacted from the settlers. I was advised by Sir John Cockburn, to whom I applied on the subject, to appeal to the legislature for relief. We did so; and though McCormick was able, by the aid of his friends, to defeat us for one year, yet we succeeded the next, upon a second appeal, and were freed from all rent thereafter, so long as we remained. Still, this was not our own land. The government, though it demanded no rent, might set up the land for sale at any time, and then we should, probably, be driven off by wealthier purchasers, with the entire loss of all our improvements, and with no retreat provided. It was manifest that it was altogether better for us to purchase before competition was invited; and we kept this fully in mind during the time we stayed here. We remained in this position six or seven years; and all this while the colored population was increasing rapidly around us, and spreading very fast into the interior settlements and the large towns. The immigration from the United Sates was incessant, and some, I am not unwilling to admit, were brought hither with my knowledge and connivance; and I will now proceed to give a short account of the plans and operations I had arranged for the liberation of some of my brethren, which I hope may prove interesting to the reader.

CHAPTER SIXTEEN

CONDUCTING SLAVES TO CANADA

Sympathy for the slaves • James Lightfoot • My first mission to the
South • A Kentucky company of fugitives • Safe at home

THE DEGRADED AND HOPELESS CONDITION OF A SLAVE, CAN NEVER BE
properly felt by him while he remains in such a position. After I had
tasted the blessings of freedom, my mind reverted to those whom I
knew were groaning in captivity, and I at once proceeded to take measures to free as many as I could. I thought that, by using exertion,
numbers might make their escape as I did, if they had some practical
advice how to proceed.

I was once attending a very large meeting at Fort Erie, at which a
great many colored people were present. In the course of my preaching I tried to impress upon them the importance of the obligations
they were under; first, to God, for their deliverance; and then, sec-
ondly, to their fellowmen, to do all that was in their power to bring
others out of bondage. In the congregation was a man named James
Lightfoot, who was of a very active temperament, and had obtained his
freedom by fleeing to Canada, but had never thought of his family and
friends whom he had left behind, until the time he heard me speaking, although he himself had been free for some five years. However,
that day the cause was brought home to his heart. When the service
was concluded he begged to have an interview with me, to which I
gladly acceded, and an arrangement was made for further conversation on the same subject one week from that time. He then informed

me where he came from, also to whom he belonged, and that he had left behind a dear father and mother, three sisters and four brothers; and that they lived on the Ohio River, not far from the city of Maysville. He said that he never saw his duty towards them to be so clear and unmistakeable as he did at that time, and professed himself ready to coöperate in any measures that might be devised for their release. During the short period of his freedom he had accumulated some little property, the whole of which, he stated, he would cheerfully devote to carrying out those measures; for he had not had any rest, night nor day, since the meeting above mentioned.

I was not able at that time to propose what was best to be done, and thus we parted; but in a few days he came to see me again on the same errand. Seeing the agony of his heart in behalf of his kindred, I consented to commence the painful and dangerous task of endeavoring to free those whom he so much loved. I left my own family in the hands of no other save God, and commenced the journey alone, on foot, and travelled thus about four hundred miles. But the Lord furnished me with strength sufficient for the undertaking. I passed through the States of New York, Pennsylvania, and Ohio—free States, so called—and crossed the Ohio River into Kentucky, and ultimately found his friends in the place he had described.

I was an entire stranger to them, but I took with me a small token of their brother who was gone, which they at once recognized; and this was to let them know that he had gone to Canada, the land of freedom, and had now sent a friend to assist them in making their escape. This created no little excitement. But his parents had become so far advanced in years that they could not undertake the fatigue; his sisters had a number of children, and they could not travel; his four brothers and a nephew were young men, and sufficiently able for the journey, but the thought of leaving their father, and mother, and sisters, was too painful; and they also considered it unsafe to make the attempt then, for fear that the excitement and grief of their friends might betray them; so they declined going at that time, but promised that they would go in a year, if I would return for them.

To this I assented, and then went between forty and fifty miles into the interior of Kentucky, having heard that there was a large party ready to attempt their escape, if they had a leader to direct their movements. I travelled by night, resting by day, and at length reached Bourbon County, the place where I expected to find these people. After a delay of about a week, spent in discussing plans, making arrangements, and other matters, I found that there, were about thirty collected from different States, who were disposed to make the attempt. At length, on a Saturday night, we started. The, agony of parting can be better conceived than described; as, in their case, husbands were leaving their wives, mothers their children, and children their parents. This, at first sight, will appear strange, and even incredible; but, when we take into consideration the fact, that at any time they were liable to be separated, by being sold to what are termed "nigger traders," and the probability that such an event would take place, it will, I think, cease to excite any surprise.

We succeeded in crossing the Ohio River in safety, and arrived in Cincinnati the third night after our departure. Here we procured assistance; and, after stopping a short time to rest, we started for Richmond, Indiana. This is a town which had been settled by Quakers, and there we found friends indeed, who at once helped us on our way, without loss of time; and after a difficult journey of two weeks, through the wilderness, we reached Toledo, Ohio, a town on the southwestern shore of Lake Erie, and there we took passage for Canada, which we reached in safety. I then went home to my family, taking with me a part of this large party, the rest finding their friends scattered in other towns, perfectly satisfied with my conduct in the matter, in being permitted to be the instrument of freeing such a number of my fellow-creatures.

CHAPTER SEVENTEEN

SECOND JOURNEY ON THE
UNDERGROUND RAILROAD

A shower of stars • Kentuckians • A stratagem • A providence
• Conducted across the Miami River by a cow • Arrival at Cincinnati
• One of the party taken ill • We leave him to die • Meet a "friend"
• A poor white man • A strange impression • Once more in Canada

I REMAINED AT HOME, WORKING ON MY FARM, UNTIL THE NEXT AUTUMN, soon after which time I had promised to assist in the restoring to liberty the friends of James Lightfoot, the individual who had excited my sympathy at the meeting at Fort Erie. In pursuance of this promise, I again started on my long journey into Kentucky.

On my way, that strange occurrence happened, called the great meteoric shower. The heavens seemed broken up into streaks of light and falling stars. I reached Lancaster, Ohio, about three o'clock in the morning, and found the village aroused, and the bells ringing, and the people exclaiming, "The day of judgment is come!" I thought it was probably so; but felt that I was in the right business, and walked on through the village, leaving the terrified people behind. The stars continued to fall till the light of the sun appeared.

On arriving at Portsmouth, in the State of Ohio, I had a very narrow escape from being detected. The place was frequented by a number of Kentuckians, who were quite ready to suspect a colored man, if they saw anything unusual about him. I reached Portsmouth in the morning, and waited until two in the afternoon for the steamboat, so that I might not arrive in Maysville till after dark. While in the town I was obliged to resort to a stratagem, in order to avoid being questioned by the Kentuckians I saw in the place. To this end I procured some dried leaves, put them into a cloth and bound it all round my face, reaching nearly to my eyes, and pretended to be so seriously affected in my head and teeth as not to be able to speak. I then hung around the village till time for the evening boat, so as to arrive at Maysville in the night. I was accosted by several during my short stay in Portsmouth, who appeared very anxious to get some particulars from me as to who I was, where I was going, and to whom I belonged. To all their numerous inquiries I merely shook my head, mumbled out indistinct answers, and acted so that they could not get anything out of me; and, by this artifice, I succeeded in avoiding any unpleasant consequences. I got on board the boat and reached Maysville, Kentucky, in the evening, about a fortnight from the time I had left Canada.

On landing a wonderful providence happened to me. The second person I met in the street was Jefferson Lightfoot, brother of the James Lightfoot previously mentioned, and one of the party who had promised to escape if I would assist them. He stated that they were still determined to make the attempt, and the following Saturday night was named to put it into execution, and preparations for the journey were at once commenced. The reason why Saturday night was chosen on this and the previous occasion was, that from not having to labor the next day, and being allowed to visit their families, they would not be missed until the time came for their usual appearance in the field, at which period they would be some eighty or a hundred miles away. During the interval I had to keep myself concealed by day, and used to meet them by night to make the necessary arrangements.

For fear of being detected, they started off without bidding their father or mother farewell, and then, in order to prevent the hounds from following on our trail, we seized a skiff, a little below the city, and made our way down the river. It was not the shortest way, but it was the surest.

It was sixty-five miles from Maysville to Cincinnati, and we thought we could reach that city before daylight, and then take the stage for Sandusky. Our boat sprung a leak before we had got half way, and we narrowly escaped being drowned; providentially, however, we got to the shore before the boat sunk. We then took another boat, but this detention prevented us from arriving at Cincinnati in time for the stage. Day broke upon us when we were about ten miles above the city, and we were compelled to leave our boat from fear of being apprehended. This was an anxious time. However, we had got so far away that we knew there was no danger of being discovered by the hounds, and we thought we would go on foot. When we got within seven miles of Cincinnati, we came to the Miami River, and we could not reach the city without crossing it.

This was a great barrier to us, for the water appeared to be deep, and we were afraid to ask the loan of a boat, being apprehensive it might lead to our detection. We went first up and then down the river, trying to find a convenient crossing place, but failed. I then said to my company, "Boys, let us go up the river and try again." We started, and after going about a mile we saw a cow coming out of a wood, and going to the river as though she intended to drink. Then said I, "Boys, let us go and see what that cow is about, it may be that she will tell us some news." I said this in order to cheer them up. One of them replied, in rather a peevish way, "Oh that cow can't talk"; but I again urged them to come on. The cow remained until we approached her within a rod or two; she then walked into the river, and went straight across without swimming, which caused me to remark, "The Lord sent that cow to show us where to cross the river!" This has always seemed to me to be a very wonderful event.

Having urged our way with considerable haste, we were literally saturated with perspiration, though it was snowing at the time, and my companions thought that it would be highly dangerous for us to proceed through the water, especially as there was a large quantity of ice in the river. But as it was a question of life or death with us, there was no time left for reasoning; I therefore advanced—they reluctantly following. The youngest of the Lightfoots ere we had reached midway of the river, was seized with violent contraction of the limbs, which prevented further self-exertion on his part; he was, therefore, carried the remainder of the distance. After resorting to continued friction, he partially recovered, and we proceeded on our journey.

We reached Cincinnati about eleven on Sunday morning—too late for the stage that day; but having found some friends, we hid ourselves until Monday evening, when we recommenced our long and toilsome journey, through mud, rain, and snow, towards Canada. We had increased our distance about 100 miles, by going out of our road to get among the Quakers. During our passage through the woods, the boy before referred to was taken alarmingly ill, and we were compelled to proceed with him on our backs; but finding this mode of conveying him exceedingly irksome, we constructed a kind of litter with our shirts and handkerchiefs laid across poles. By this time we got into the State of Indiana, so that we could travel by day as long as we kept to the woods. Our patient continued to get worse, and it appeared, both to himself and to us all, that death would soon release him from his sufferings. He therefore begged to be left in some secluded spot, to die alone, as he feared that the delay occasioned by his having to be carried through the bush, might lead to the capture of the whole company. With very considerable reluctance we acceded to his request, and laid him in a sheltered place, with a full expectation that death would soon put an end to his sufferings. The poor fellow expressed his readiness to meet the last struggle in hope of eternal life. Sad, indeed, was the parting; and it was with difficulty we tore ourselves away.

We had not, however, proceeded more than two miles on our journey, when one of the brothers of the dying man made a sudden stop, and expressed his inability to proceed whilst he had the consciousness that he had left his brother to perish, in all probability, a prey to the devouring wolves. His grief was so great that we determined to return, and at length reached the spot, where we found the poor fellow apparently dying, moaning out with every breath a prayer to heaven. Words cannot describe the joyousness experienced by the Lightfoots when they saw their poor afflicted brother once more; they literally danced for joy. We at once prepared to resume our journey as we best could, and once more penetrated the bush. After making some progress, we saw, at a little distance on the road, a wagon approaching, and I immediately determined to ascertain whether some assistance could not be obtained.

I at length circumvented the road, so as to make it appear that I had been journeying in an opposite direction to that which the wagon was taking. When I came up with the driver, I bade him good day. He said, "Where is thee going?" "To Canada." I saw his coat, heard his *thee* and *thou,* and set him down for a Quaker. I therefore plainly told him our circumstances. He at once stopped his horses, and expressed his willingness to assist us. I returned to the place where my companions were in waiting for me, and soon had them in the presence of the Quaker. Immediately on viewing the sufferer he was moved to tears, and without delay turned his horses' heads, to proceed in the direction of his home, although he had intended to go to a distant market with a load of produce for sale. The reception we met with from the Quaker's family overjoyed our hearts, and the transports with which the poor men looked upon their brother, now so favorably circumstanced, cannot be described.

We remained with this happy family for the night, and received from them every kindness. It was arranged that the boy should remain behind until, through the blessing of God, he should recover. We were kindly provided by them with a sack of biscuit and a joint of meat, and once more set our faces in the direction of Lake Erie.

After proceeding some distance on our road, we perceived a white man approaching, but as he was travelling alone, and on foot, we were not alarmed at his presence. It turned out that he had been residing for some time in the South, and although a free man, his employers had attempted to castigate him; in return for which he had used violence, which made it necessary that he should at once escape. We travelled in company, and found that his presence was of signal service to us in delivering us out of the hands of the slave-hunters who were now on our track, and eagerly grasping after their prey. We had resolved on reaching the lake, a distance of forty miles, by the following morning; we, therefore, walked all night.

Just as the day was breaking, we reached a wayside tavern, immediately contiguous to the lake, and our white companion having knocked up the landlord, ordered breakfast for six. Whilst our breakfast was in course of preparation, we dosed off into slumber, wearied with our long-continued exertion.

Just as our breakfast was ready, whilst half asleep and half awake, an impression came forcibly upon me that danger was nigh, and that I must at once leave the house. I immediately urged my companions to follow me out, which they were exceedingly unwilling to do; but as they had promised me submission, they at length yielded to my request. We retired to the yard at the side of the house, and commenced washing ourselves with the snow, which was now up to our knees. Presently we heard the tramping of horses, and were at once warned of the necessity of secreting ourselves. We crept beneath a pile of bushes which were lying close at hand, which permitted a full view of the road. The horsemen came to a dead stop at the door of the house, and commenced their inquiries; my companions at once recognized the parties on horseback, and whispered their names to me. This was a critical moment, and the loud beatings of their hearts testified the dreadful alarm with which they viewed the scene. Had we been within doors, we should have been inevitably sacrificed. Our white friend proceeded to the door in advance of the landlord, and maintained his position. He was at once interrogated by the slave-hunters whether he had seen any negroes pass that way. He said, yes, he thought he had. Their number was demanded, and they were told about six, and that they were proceeding in the direction of Detroit; and that they might be some few miles on the road. They at once reined their horses, which were greatly fatigued, through having been ridden all night, and were soon out of sight. We at length ventured into the house, and devoured breakfast in an incredibly short space of time. After what had transpired, the landlord became acquainted with our circumstances, and at once offered to sail us in his boat across to Canada. We were happy enough to have such an offer, and soon the white sail of our little bark was laying to the wind, and we were gliding along on our way, with the land of liberty in full view. Words cannot describe the feelings experienced by my companions as they neared the shore; their bosoms were swelling with inexpressible joy as they mounted the seats of the boat, ready, eagerly, to spring forward, that they might touch the soil of the freeman. And when they reached the shore, they danced and wept for joy, and kissed the earth on which they first stepped, no longer the SLAVE—but the FREE.

After the lapse of a few months, on one joyous Sabbath morning, I had the happiness of clasping the poor boy we had left in the kind care of the Quaker, no longer attenuated in frame, but robust and healthy, and surrounded by his family. Thus my joy was consummated, and superadded was the blessing of those who were ready to perish, which came upon me. It is one of the greatest sources of my happiness to know, that by similar means to those above narrated, I have been instrumental in delivering *one hundred and eighteen* human beings out of the cruel and merciless grasp of the slaveholder.

Mr. Frank Taylor, the owner of the Lightfoots, whose escape I have just narrated, soon after he missed his slaves, fell ill, and became quite deranged; but, on recovering, he was persuaded by his friends to free the remainder of the family of the Lightfoots, which he at length did; and, after a short lapse of time, they all met each other in Canada, where they are now living.

CHAPTER EIGHTEEN

HOME AT DAWN

Condition in Canada • Efforts in behalf of my people
• Rev. Mr. Wilson • A convention of blacks • Manual-labor school

I DID NOT FIND THAT OUR PROSPERITY INCREASED WITH OUR NUMBERS. The mere delight the slave took in his freedom, rendered him, at first, contented with a lot far inferior to that which he might have attained. Then his ignorance led him to make unprofitable bargains, and he would often hire wild land on short terms, and bind himself to clear a certain number of acres; and by the time they were clear and fitted for cultivation, his lease was out, and his landlord would come in, and raise a splendid crop on the new land; and the tenant would, very likely, start again on just such another bargain, and be no better off at the end of ten years than he was at the beginning. Another way in which they lost the profits of their labor was by raising nothing but tobacco, the high price of which was very tempting, and the cultivation of which was a monopoly in their hands, as no white man understood it, or could compete with them at all. The consequence was, however, that they had nothing but tobacco to sell; there was rather too much of it in the market, and the price of wheat rose, while their commodity was depressed; and they lost all they should have saved, in the profit they gave the trader for his corn and stores.

I saw the effect of these things so clearly that I could not help trying to make my friends and neighbors see it too; and I set seriously about the business of lecturing upon the subject of crops, wages, and profit, just as if I had been brought up to it. I insisted on the necessity of their raising their own crops, saving their own wages, and securing the profits of their own labor, with such plain arguments as occurred to me, and were as clear to their comprehension as to mine. I did this very openly; and, frequently, my audience consisted in part of the very traders whose inordinate profits upon individuals I was trying to diminish, but whose balance of profit would not be ultimately lessened, because they would have so many more persons to trade with, who would be able to pay them a reasonable advance in cash, or its equivalent, on all their purchases. The purse is a tender part of the system; but I handled it so gently, that the sensible portion of my natural opponents were not, I believe, offended; while those whom I wished to benefit saw, for the most part, the propriety of my advice, and took it. At least, there are now great numbers of settlers, in this region of Canada, who own their farms, and are training up their children in true independence, and giving them a good elementary education, who had not taken a single step towards such a result before I began to talk to them.

While I remained at Colchester, I became acquainted with a Congregational missionary from Massachusetts, by the name of Hiram Wilson, who took an interest in our people, and was disposed to do what he could to promote the cause of improvement which I had so much at heart. He coöperated with me in many efforts, and I have been associated with him from 1836 to the present time. He has been a faithful friend, and still continues his important labors of love in our behalf. Among other things which he did for us then, he wrote to a Quaker friend of his, an Englishman, by the name of James C. Fuller, residing at Skencateles, New York, and endeavored to interest him in the welfare of our struggling population.

He succeeded so far, that Mr. Fuller, who was going on a visit to England, promised to do what he could among his friends there, to induce them to aid us. He came back with fifteen hundred dollars which had been subscribed for our benefit. It was a great question how this sum, which sounded vast to many of my brethren, should be appropriated. I had my own opinion pretty decidedly as to what it was best for us all to do with it. But, in order to come to a satisfactory conclusion, the first thing to be done was to call a convention of delegates from every settlement of blacks that was within reach; that all might see that whatever was decided on, was sanctioned by the disinterested votes of those who were thought by their companions, best able to judge what was expedient. Mr. Wilson and myself called such a convention, therefore, to meet in London, Upper Canada, and it was held in June, 1838.

I urged the appropriation of the money to the establishment of a manual-labor school, where our children could be taught those elements of knowledge which are usually the occupations of a grammar-school; and where the boys could be taught, in addition, the practice of some mechanic art, and the girls could be instructed in those domestic arts which are the proper occupation and ornament of their sex. Such an establishment would train up those who would afterwards instruct others; and we should thus gradually become independent of the white man for our intellectual progress, as we might be also for our physical prosperity. It was the more necessary, as in many districts, owing to the insurmountable prejudices of the inhabitants, the children of the blacks were not allowed to share the advantages of the common school. There was some opposition to this plan in the convention; but in the course of the discussion, which continued for three days, it appeared so obviously for the advantage of all to husband this donation, so as to preserve it for a purpose of permanent utility, that the proposal was, at last, unanimously adopted; and a committee of three was appointed to select and purchase a sight for the establishment. Mr. Wilson and myself were the active members of this committee, and after traversing the country for several months, we could find no place more suitable than that upon which I had had my eye for three or four years, for a permanent settlement, in the town of Dawn.

We therefore bought two hundred acres of fine rich land, on the river Sydenham, covered with a heavy growth of black walnut and white wood, at four dollars the acre. I had made a bargain for two hundred acres adjoining this lot, on my own account; and circumstances favored me so, that the man of whom I purchased was glad to let me have them at a large discount from the price I had agreed to pay, if I would give him cash for the balance I owed him. I transferred a portion of the advantage of this bargain to the institution, by selling to it one hundred acres more, at the low price at which I obtained them.

In 1842 I removed with my family to Dawn, and as a considerable number of my friends are there about me, and the school is permanently fixed there, the future importance of this settlement seems to be decided. There are many other settlements which are considerable; and, indeed, the colored population is scattered over a territory which does not fall far short of three hundred miles in extent, in each direction, and probably numbers not less than twenty thousand persons in all. We look to the school, and the possession of landed property by individuals, as two great means of the elevation of our oppressed and degraded race to a participation in the blessings, as they have hitherto been permitted to share only the miseries and vices, of civilization.

My efforts to aid them, in every way in my power, and to procure the aid of others for them, have been constant. I have made many journeys into New York, Connecticut, Massachusetts, and Maine, in all of which States I have found or made some friends to the cause, and, I hope, some personal friends. I have received many liberal gifts, and experienced much kindness of treatment; but I must be allowed to allude particularly to the donations received from Boston—by which we have been enabled to erect a sawmill, and thus to begin in good earnest the clearing of our lands, and to secure a profitable return for the support of our school—as among those which have been most welcome and valuable to us.

Some of the trips I have made, have led to some incidents and observations which must be the theme of a future chapter.

CHAPTER NINETEEN

LUMBERING OPERATIONS

Industrial project • Find some able friends in Boston
• Procure funds and construct a sawmill • Sales of lumber
in Boston • Incident in the Custom House

THE LAND ON WHICH WE SETTLED IN CANADA WAS COVERED WITH A beautiful forest of noble trees of various kinds. Our people were accustomed to cut them down and burn them on the ground, simply to get rid of them. Often as I roamed through the forest, I was afflicted at seeing such waste, and longed to devise some means of converting this abundant natural wealth into money, so as to improve the condition of the people.

Full of this subject, I left my home on a journey of observation through the State of New York, and New England. I kept my purposes to myself, not breathing a word of my intentions to any mortal. I found in New York, mills where precisely such logs as those in Canada were sawed into lumber, which I learned commanded large prices. In New England I found a ready market for the black walnut, white wood, and other lumber, such as abounded and was wasted in Canada.

On reaching Boston, Mass. I made known these facts and my feelings to some philanthropic gentlemen with whom I had become acquainted. It cannot be improper for me to mention the names of these gentlemen, who lent so ready an ear to my representations, and placed so much confidence in my judgment, as to furnish me with the means of starting what has since proved a very profitable enterprise.

Rev. Ephraim Peabody introduced me to Samuel Eliot, Esq., who was kind enough to examine carefully into all my representations, and to draw up a sketch of them, which was afterwards presented to Amos Lawrence, Esq., and others. By means of this a collection of money to aid me was made, to which many of the leading gentleman of Boston contributed, amounting to about fourteen hundred dollars.

With this money I returned to Canada, and immediately set myself about building a sawmill in Camden (then Dawn). The improvement in the surrounding section was astonishing. The people began to labor, and the progress in clearing up and cultivating the land was quite cheering.

But after the framework of my mill was completed and covered, my scanty funds were exhausted. This was a trying time. I had begun the work in faith, I had expended the money honestly, and to the best of my judgment, and now should the whole enterprise fail? I immediately returned to my Boston friends. Amos Lawrence, H. Ingersoll Bowditch, and Samuel A. Elliot, Esqs., listened to me again, and gave me to understand that they deemed me an honest man. They encouraged me in my business enterprise, and the approval of such men was like balm to my soul. They endorsed a note for me and put it into the bank, by which I was enabled to borrow, on my own responsibility, about eighteen hundred dollars more. With this I soon completed the mill, stocked it with machinery, and had the pleasure of seeing it in successful operation. I ought here to add, that the mill was not my own private property, but belonged to an association, which established an excellent manual-labor school, where many children and youth of both sexes have been educated. The school was well attended by both colored children, whites, and some Indians.

This enterprise having been completed to a great extent by my own labor and the labor of my own sons, who took charge of the mill, I immediately began to consider how I could discharge my pecuniary obligations. I chartered a vessel, and loaded it with eighty thousand feet of good prime black walnut lumber, sawed in our mill, and contracted with the captain to deliver it for me at Oswego, N. Y. I entered into a contract there with a party to have it delivered at Boston, but the party having forwarded it to New York, failed to carry it any farther.

There great efforts were made to cheat me out of the lumber, but, by the good friendship of Mr. Lawrence, of Boston, who furnished me the means of having it reshipped, I succeeded in bringing the whole eighty thousand feet safe to Boston, where I sold it to Mr. Jonas Chickering for forty-five dollars per thousand feet. The proceeds paid all expenses, and would have cancelled all the debts I had incurred; but my friends insisted that I should retain a part of the funds for future use. After that, I brought another large load of lumber by the same route.

The next season I brought a large cargo by the river St. Lawrence, which came direct to Boston, where, without the aid of any agent or third party whatever, I paid my own duties, got the lumber through the Custom House, and sold it at a handsome profit. A little incident occurred when paying the duties, which has often since afforded me a great deal of amusement. The Fugitive Slave Law had just been passed in the United States, which made it quite an offence to harbor or render aid to a fugitive slave. When the Custom House officer presented his bill to me for the duties on my lumber, I jokingly remarked to him that perhaps he would render himself liable to trouble if he should have dealings with a fugitive slave, and if so I would relieve him of the trouble of taking my money. "Are you a fugitive slave, Sir?" "Yes, Sir," said I; "and perhaps you had better not have any dealings with me." "I have nothing to do with that," said the official; "there is your bill. You have acted like a man, and I deal with you as a man." I enjoyed the scene, and the bystanders seemed to relish it, and I paid him the money.

I look back upon the enterprise related in this chapter with a great deal of pleasure, for the mill which was then built introduced an entire change in the appearance of that section of the country, and in the habits of the people.

CHAPTER TWENTY

Visit to England

Debt on the institution • A new pecuniary enterprise
• Letters of recommendation to England • Personal difficulties
• Called an imposter • Triumphant victory over these troubles

MY INTEREST IN THE MANUAL LABOR SCHOOL IN DAWN, WAS THE means of my visiting England. No one who has never engaged in such business can have any idea of the many difficulties connected with so great an enterprise. In spite of all the efforts of the Association, a debt of about seven thousand five hundred dollars rested upon it. A meeting of its trustees and friends, in the year 1849, was called to consider its condition, and to devise, if possible, some means for its relief. After a long discussion of the matter, it was finally determined to separate the concern into two departments, and put it under the charge of two parties, the one to take the mill and a certain portion of the land for four years, and to pay all the debts of the institution in that time; and the other party to take the other buildings and land, and to conduct the school.

A certain party was found willing to assume the school. But who would be enterprising enough to take the mill for four years encumbered with a debt of seven thousand five hundred dollars was a very important question.

On consideration, having a secret project in my own mind, I concluded to do it, provided that Mr. Peter B. Smith would assume an equal share of the responsibility, and attend to the business of the mill. He readily consented.

My project was to go to England, carrying with me some of the best specimens of black walnut boards our farm would produce, and to exhibit them in the great World's Industrial Exhibition, then in session at London, and perhaps negotiate for the sale of lumber. I accordingly left for England, being readily furnished with very complimentary letters of introduction to such men as Thomas Binney, Samuel Gurney, Lord Brougham, Hon. Abbot Lawrence, then American Minister to England, from Rev. John Rolfe, of Toronto, Chief Justice Robinson, Sir Allen McNab, Col. John Prince, Rev. Dr. Duffield, of Detroit, Michigan, Judge Conant, of the same city, Hon. Ross Wilkinson, U. S. Judge, residing also in Detroit, Hon. Charles Sumner and Amos Lawrence, Esq., of Massachusetts. From the gentlemen above mentioned I had in England a most cordial reception, and was immediately introduced to the very best society in the kingdom.

I regret exceedingly to make any allusions to personal difficulties, or to individuals that have pursued an unjust and unchristian course towards me or others, but I cannot give anything like a correct view of this part of my history without, at least, a brief allusion, which shall be as delicate as I can make it, to some difficulties.

It was undoubtedly the plan of certain individuals of the party who assumed the care of the school, probably from unworthy sectarian feelings, to obtain entire possession of the property of the association, or certainly, completely to destroy my influence over it, and connection with it.

Much to my astonishment, therefore, when I had arrived in England, and had been cordially received by the men above mentioned, and had preached in the pulpits of such men as Rev. Messrs. Thomas Binney, Baptist Noel, William Brock, James Sherman, George Smith, Dr. Burns, in London, and had already introduced my enterprise before a portion of the British public, I was confronted by a printed and published circular, to the following effect: "That one styling himself Rev. Josiah Henson was an impostor, obtaining money under false pretences; that he could exhibit no good credentials; that whatever money he might obtain would not be appropriated according to the wish of the donors, and that the said Josiah Henson was an artful, skilful, and eloquent man, and would probably deceive the public."

This was a severe blow, but fortunately I had already requested my friends to appoint a committee of twelve persons to examine carefully into the merits of my enterprise, which committee should appoint a subcommittee of three, and a treasurer, to receive every farthing contributed to me by the public, and to appropriate it only as they should deem proper. This committee had been appointed, and consisted of Samuel Gurney, Samuel Gurney, Junior, Samuel Marley, Esq., George Hitchcock, Esq., Rev. James Sherman, Rev. Thomas Binney, Rev. John Branch, Eusebius Smith, Esq., John Scobell, Secretary of the British and Foreign Antislavery Society, Lord Ashley (now Earl of Shaftsbury), George Sturge, and Thomas Sturge. The subcommittee of three were, John Scobell, Rev. John Branch, and Eusebius Smith, who appointed Samuel Gurney, Junior, treasurer. Many of the above names are known throughout the world.

When the above attack was made upon me, a meeting of those interested in my cause was called, and my accuser, who was in the country, was requested to meet me face to face.

I forbear to mention his name, or to describe particularly the sources of this trouble, because I do not wish to injure the feelings of any person. The name, however, I can at any time give. I believe all the difficulty arose from little petty jealousies, fostered, perhaps, by the unworthy influences of slavery, over the misguided people who were for a time misled by false representations.

We met before a company of English gentlemen, who heard all that my accuser had to say. They asked me for a reply. I simply restated to them all the facts I had previously made known. I reminded them that a man who devotes himself to do good, must and will be misunderstood and have enemies. I called their attention to the misinterpretation of their own motives made by their enemies. I then related to them the parable of Christ about the wheat and the tares. My recommendatory letters were reread—a sufficient reply to the allegation that I was an impostor.

They were pleased to assure me of their entire satisfaction; but to give perfect quiet to the public they determined, at their own expense, to send an agent to Canada, to make a full inquiry into the matter, and advised me to accompany him. Accordingly John Scobell and myself started for Canada immediately. I had already collected nearly seventeen hundred dollars, which, of course, remained in the hands of the treasurer.

A mass meeting, of all interested in the matter, was called in the institution on the premises. A large assemblage met, and Rev. John Rolfe of Toronto, presided. A thorough examination into the records of the institution was made. The originator of the slander against me denied having made it; it was proved upon him, and the whole convention unanimously repudiated the false charges. Mr. Scobell remained in Canada about three months, and before leaving, sent me a letter, informing me that whenever I should see fit to return to England, I should find in the hands of Amos Lawrence, Esq., of Boston, a draft to defray the expenses of the journey. Accordingly, in the latter part of 1851, I returned.

The ground was now prepared for me, and I reaped an abundant harvest. The whole debt of the institution was cancelled in a few months, when I was recalled to Canada by the fatal illness of my wife. Several very interesting occurrences happened during my stay in England, which I must relate in another chapter.

→ CHAPTER TWENTY-ONE ←

THE WORLD'S FAIR IN LONDON

My contribution to the great exhibition • Difficulty with the
American superintendent • Happy release • The great crowd
• A call from the Queen • Medal awarded to me

I HAVE ALREADY MENTIONED THAT THE FIRST IDEA WHICH SUGGESTED
to me the plan of going to England, was to exhibit, at the Great
World's Fair, in London, some of the best specimens of our black
walnut lumber, in the hope that it might lead to some sales in England. For this purpose I selected some of the best boards out of the
cargo which I had brought to Boston, which Mr. Chickering was kind
enough to have properly packed in boxes, and sent to England in the
American ship which carried the American products for exhibition.
The boards which I selected were four in number, excellent specimens, about seven feet in length and four feet in width, of beautiful
grain and texture. On their arrival in England, I had them planed
and perfectly polished, in French style, so that they actually shone
like a mirror.

The history of my connection with the World's Fair is a little amus-
ing. Because my boards happened to be carried over in the American
ship, the superintendent of the American Department, who was from
Boston, (I think his name was Riddle), insisted that my lumber should
be exhibited in the American department. To this I objected. I was a
citizen of Canada, and my boards were from Canada, and there was
an apartment of the building appropriated to Canadian products. I

therefore insisted that my boards should be removed from the American Department, to the Canadian. But, said the American, "You cannot do it. All these things are under my control. You can exhibit what belongs to you if you please, but not a single thing here must be moved an inch without my consent."

This was rather a damper to me. I thought his position was rather absurd, but how to move him or my boards seemed just then beyond my control.

A happy thought, however, occurred to me. Thought I, if this Yankee wants to retain my furniture, the world shall know who it belongs to. I accordingly hired a painter to paint in good large white letters on the tops of my boards: "THIS IS THE PRODUCT OF THE INDUSTRY OF A FUGITIVE SLAVE FROM THE UNITED STATES, WHOSE RESIDENCE IS DAWN, CANADA." This was done early in the morning. In due time the American superintendent came around, and found me at my post. The gaze of astonishment with which he read my inscription, was laughable to witness. His face was black as a thunder-cloud. "Look here, Sir," said he; "What, under heaven, have you got up there?" "O, that is only a little information to let the people know who I am." "But don't you know better than that. Do you suppose I am going to have that insult up there?" The English gentlemen began to gather around, chuckling with half-suppressed delight, to see the wrath of the Yankee. This only added fuel to the fire. "Well, Sir," said he, "do you suppose I am going to bring that stuff across the Atlantic for nothing?" "I have never asked you to bring it for nothing. I am ready to pay you, and have been from the beginning." "Well, Sir, you may take it away, and carry it where you please." "O," said I, "I think, as you wanted it very much, I will not disturb it. You can have it now." "No, Sir; take it away!" "I beg your pardon, Sir," said I, "when I wanted to remove it you would not allow it, and now, for all me, it shall remain." In the meantime the crowd enjoyed it and so did I. The result was, that by the next day the boards were removed to their proper place at no expense to me, and no bill was ever presented against me for carrying the lumber across the Atlantic.

I may be permitted to say that in that immense exhibition, my humble contribution received its due share of attention. Many conversations did I have with individuals of that almost innumerable multitude from every nation under heaven. Perhaps my complexion attracted attention, but nearly all who passed, paused to look at me, and at themselves as reflected in my large black walnut mirrors.

Among others the Queen of England, Victoria, preceded by her guide, and attended by her cortége, paused to view me and my property. I uncovered my head and saluted her as respectfully as I could, and she was pleased with perfect grace to return my salutation. "Is he indeed a fugitive slave?" I heard her inquire; and the answer was, "He is indeed, and that is his work."

But notwithstanding such pleasant occurrences, the time wore heavily away. The immense crowd, kept in as perfect order as a single family, became wearisome to me, and I was not sorry, as related in a preceding chapter, to return to Canada, leaving my boards on exhibition.

On going again to England the exhibition was still in progress. There seemed no diminution of the crowd. Like the waters of the great Mississippi, the channel was still full, though the individuals were changed.

But among all the exhibitors from every nation in Europe, and from Asia, and America, and the Isles of the Sea, there was not a single black man but myself. There were negroes there from Africa, brought to be exhibited, but no exhibitors but myself. Though my condition was wonderfully changed from what it was in my childhood and youth, yet it was a little saddening to reflect that my people were not more largely represented there. The time will yet come, I trust, when such a state of things will no longer exist.

At the close of the exhibition, on my return to Canada, I received from England a large quarto bound volume containing a full description of all the objects presented at the exhibition, the names of officers of all the committees, juries, exhibitors, prizes, etc., etc. Among others I found my own name recorded; and there were in addition awarded to me a bronze medal, a beautiful picture of the Queen and royal family, of the size of life, and several other objects of interest.

These things I greatly prize. After having fully succeeded in my mission to England, having released myself from the voluntarily assumed debt in behalf of the manual-labor school, and having received these testimonials of honor, I returned home to Canada, contented and happy. While in England I was permitted to enjoy some excellent opportunities to witness its best society, which I propose to relate in the following chapter.

CHAPTER TWENTY-TWO

Visits to the Ragged Schools

Speech at Sunday School Anniversary • Interview with Lord Grey
• Interview with the Archbishop of Canterbury, and dinner with
Lord John Russell, the great events of my life

While in England I was frequently called upon to speak at public meetings of various kinds. I was deeply interested in the Ragged School enterprise, and frequently addressed the schools, and also public meetings held in their behalf. I spent two months of May, in that country, and attended many of the great anniversaries, and was called upon to speak at many of them. On several occasions I did what I could to make known the true condition of slaves, in Exeter Hall and other places. On one occasion, I recollect, an eminent man from Pennsylvania was addressing the anniversary of a Sabbath School Union, who boasted of the great benefits of Sunday Schools in the United States, and asserted that all classes indiscriminately enjoyed their blessings. I felt bound to contradict him, and after putting to the speaker a few questions which he stammeringly answered, I told the immense meeting that in the Southern States, the great body of the colored people were almost entirely neglected, and in many places they were excluded altogether; and that even in the most of the Northern States, the great mass of the colored children were not sought out and gathered into Sunday Schools. This created some little storm, but my own personal observation and experience carried conviction to the people.

Being thus introduced to the public, I became well acquainted with many of the leading men of England. Lord Grey made a proposition to me, which, if circumstances had permitted, I should have been glad to attempt. It was to go to India and there superintend some great efforts made by the government to introduce the culture of cotton on the American plan. He promised to me an appointment to an office, and a good salary. Had it not been for my warm interest in my Canadian enterprise, I should have accepted his proposal.

One of the most pleasing incidents for me now to look back upon, was a long interview which I was permitted to enjoy with the Archbishop of Canterbury. The elevated social position of this man, the highest beneath the crown, is well known to all those acquainted with English society. Samuel Gurney, the noted philanthropist, introduced me, by a note and his family card, to his grace, the archbishop. He received me kindly in his palace. I immediately entered upon a conversation with him, upon the condition of my people, and the plans I had in view. He expressed the strongest interest in me, and after about a half hour's conversation he inquired, "At what university, Sir, did you graduate?" "I graduated, your grace," said I in reply, "at the university of adversity." "The university of adversity," said he, looking up with astonishment; "where is that?" I saw his surprise, and explained. "It was my lot, your grace," said I, "to be born a slave, and to pass my boyhood and all the former part of my life as a slave. I never entered a school, never read the Bible in my youth, and received all of my training under the most adverse circumstances. This is what I meant by graduating in the university of adversity." "I understand you, Sir," said he. "But is it possible that you are not a scholar?" "I am not," said I. "But I should never have suspected that you were not a liberally educated man. I have heard many negroes talk, but have never seen one that could use such language as you. Will you tell me, Sir, how you learned our language?" I then explained to him, as well as I could, my early life; that it had always been my custom to observe good speakers, and to imitate only those who seemed to speak most correctly. "It is astonishing," said the archbishop. "And is it possible that you were brought up ignorant of religion? How did you attain to the knowledge of Christ?" I explained to him, in reply, that a poor ignorant slave mother had taught me to say the Lord's Prayer, though I did not know then how, truly, to pray. "And how were you led to a better knowledge of the Saviour?" I answered that it was by the hearing of the Gospel preached. He then asked me to repeat the text, and to explain all the circumstances. I told him of the first sermon I heard, of the text, "He, by the grace of God, tasted death for every man." "A beautiful text was that," said the archbishop, and so affected was he by my simple story that he shed tears freely.

I had been told by Samuel Gurney that perhaps the archbishop would give me an interview of a quarter of an hour; I glanced at the clock and found that I had already been there an hour and a half, and arose to depart. He followed me to the door, and begged of me if ever I came to England to call and see him again; and shaking hands affectionately with me, while the tears trembled in his eyes, he put into my hands graciously five golden sovereigns, (about twenty-five dollars), and bade me adieu. I have always esteemed him as a warmhearted Christian.

Thus ended the interview with the venerable Archbishop of England. On my second visit to England, I had an invitation, in company with a large number of Sabbath School Teachers, to spend a day on the beautiful grounds of Lord John Russell, then Prime Minister of England. His magnificent park, filled with deer, of all colors, and from all climes, and sleek hares, which the poet COWPER would have envied, with numberless birds, whose plumage rivalled the rainbow in gorgeous colors, together with the choicest specimens of the finny tribe, sporting in their native element, drew from me the involuntary exclamation: "O, how different the condition of these happy, sportive, joyful, creatures, from what was once my own condition, and what is now the lot of millions of my colored brethren in America!" This occupancy of the elegant grounds of England's Prime Minister, for the day, by a party of Sabbath School Teachers, was what we should call, in America, a picnic, with this difference, that, instead of each teacher providing his own cakes, and pies, and fruit, they were furnished by men and women, who were allowed to come on to the grounds, with every variety of choice eatables for sale. After strolling over these charming grounds, enjoying the beautiful scenery, and the happy gambols of the brute creation, and the conversation of the many intelligent men and women, with whom we came in contact, we were most unexpectedly, at five o'clock, sent for to visit the elegant mansion of the proprietor. There we found what I will call a surprise party, or at any rate, we were taken by surprise, for we were ushered, three hundred of us at least, into a spacious dining hall, whose dimensions could not have been less than one hundred feet by sixty, and here were tables, groaning under every article of luxury for the palate, which England could supply, and to this bountiful repast we were all made welcome. I was invited to take the head of the table; I never felt so highly honored. The blessing was invoked by singing the two following verses.

> Be present at our table, Lord,
> Be here and everywhere adored:
> These creatures bless,
> And grant that we may feast
> In Paradise with thee!

After dinner, various toasts were proposed, on various subjects, and in my humble way I offered the following:

First to England. Honor to the brave, freedom to the Slave, success to British emancipation. God bless the Queen!

Cheers and laughter followed the reading of this toast, succeeded by the usual English exclamations, "*Up, up, up again!*" I again arose and gave, To our most Sovereign Lady, the Queen:

May she have a long life, and a happy death. May she reign in righteousness, and rule in love!

And to her illustrious consort, Prince Albert:

May he have peace at home, pleasure abroad, love his Queen, and serve the Lord!

Among the distinguished persons who made speeches on this joyous occasion, I will mention the names of Rev. William Brock, Hon. Samuel M. Peto, and a Mr. Bess, brother-in-law of Mr. Peto, with his accomplished and beautiful lady. Thus ended one of the pleasantest days of my life.

CHAPTER TWENTY-THREE

CLOSING UP MY LONDON AGENCY

My narrative published • Letter from home apprising me of the
sickness of my wife • Departure from London • Arrival at home
• Meeting with my family • The great sorrow of my life,
the death of my wife

THE DINNER AT LORD JOHN RUSSELL'S, AS DETAILED IN THE PREVIOUS
chapter, was in the month of June, 1852; from that time to the first of
August I was busily employed in finishing up all matters connected
with my agency, in which I was very successful, having accomplished
the objects of my mission. During the month of August, I was engaged
in publishing a narrative of incidents in my slave-life, which I had been
urgently requested to do by some of the noblest men and women in
England. Just as I had completed the work, and issued an edition of
two thousand copies, I received, on the third of September, a letter
from my family in Canada, stating that my beloved wife, the companion of my life, the sharer of my joys and sorrows, lay at the point of
death, and that she earnestly desired me to return immediately, that
she might see me once more before she bid adieu to earth. This was a
trying hour for me. I was in England, four thousand miles from my
home. I had just embarked in an enterprise which I had every reason
to suppose would be a very profitable undertaking. The first edition
of my book was ready for sale, and now What shall I do? Was the question which I asked myself. Shall I remain here and sell ten thousand
copies of my book, and make a handsome sum of money for myself

and family, or shall I leave all and hasten to the bedside of my dying wife? I was not long in deciding the question. I will leave my books and stereotype plates, and all my property behind, and go. And on the morning of the fourth of September, having received the letter from home at four o'clock on the afternoon of the third, I was on my way from London to Liverpool, and embarked from Liverpool on the fifth, in the steamer Canada, bound for Boston. On the twentieth of the same month I arrived at my own Canadian home. Those who have been placed in similar situations, can realize what must have been my feelings as I drew near my humble dwelling. I had heard nothing since the information contained in the letter which reached me at Liverpool. I knew not whether my dear wife, the mother of my children, she who had travelled with me, sad and solitary, and foot-sore, from the land of bondage; who had been to me a kind, and affectionate, and dutiful wife, for forty years, I knew not whether she was still alive, or whether she had entered into rest.

A merciful Father had, however, kindly prolonged her life, and we were permitted once more to meet. And oh! Such a meeting; it was worth more to me than all the fancied gains from my English book. I was met in the yard by four of my daughters, who rushed to my arms, delighted at my unexpected return. They begged me not to go in to see mother, until they should first go and prepare her for it, thinking very wisely that the shock would be too great for her poor shattered nerves to bear. I consented that they should precede me. They immediately repaired to her sick room, and by gradual stages prepared her mind for our meeting. When I went to her bedside, she received and embraced me with the calmness and fortitude of a Christian, and even chided me for the strong emotions of sorrow which I found it utterly impossible to suppress. I found her perfectly calm and resigned to the will of God, awaiting with Christian firmness the hour for her summons. She was rejoiced to see me once more, while at the same time she said that perhaps she had done wrong in allowing me to be sent for to return, leaving my business behind, with all its flattering prospects. I told her that I was more than satisfied, that I was truly thankful to my Heavenly Father for granting us this interview, no matter what the pecuniary sacrifice might be. We talked over our whole past life as far as her strength would permit, reviewing the many scenes of sorrow and trouble, as well as the many bright and happy days of our pilgrimage, until exhausted nature sought repose, and she sunk into a quiet sleep.

The day following she revived; my return seeming to inspire her with the hope that possibly she might again be restored to health. It was not, however, so to be; but God in his mercy granted her a reprieve, and her life was prolonged a few weeks. I thus had the melancholy satisfaction of watching day and night by her bed of languishing and pain, and was permitted to close her eyes when the final summons came. She blessed me, and blessed her children, commending us to the ever watchful care of that Saviour who had sustained her in so many hours of trial; and finally, after kissing me and each one of the children, she passed from earth to heaven without a pang or a groan, as gently as the falling to sleep of an infant on its mother's breast.

> Who would not wish to die like those
> Whom God's own spirit deigns to bless?
> To sink into that soft repose,
> Then wake to perfect happiness?

I can truly and from an overflowing heart say, that she was a sincere and devoted Christian, and a faithful and kind wife to me, even up to the day of her death arranging all our domestic matters in such a manner as to contribute as largely as possible to my comfort and happiness.

Rest in peace, dear wife. If I am faithful to the end, as thou wert, we shall ere long meet again in that world where the sorrows of life shall not be remembered or brought into mind.

CHAPTER TWENTY-FOUR

CLOSING CHAPTER

Containing an accurate account of the past and present
condition of the fugitive slaves in Canada, with some remarks
on their future prospects

I HAVE BEEN REQUESTED BY MANY FRIENDS IN THIS COUNTRY TO devote a chapter of my book to the fugitive slaves in Canada; to a statement of their present numbers, condition, prospects for the future, etc. At the time of my first visit to Canada, in the year 1830, there were but a few hundred fugitive slaves in both Canadas; there are now not less than thirty-five thousand. At that time they were scattered in all directions, and for the most part miserably poor, subsisting not unfrequently on the roots and herbs of the fields; now many of them own large and valuable farms, and but few can be found in circumstances of destitution or want. In 1830 there were no schools among them, and no churches, and only occasional preaching. We have now numerous churches, and they are well filled from Sabbath to Sabbath with attentive listeners; our children attend the Sabbath School, and are being trained as we trust for Heaven. We depend principally upon our farms for subsistence, but some of our number are good mechanics—blacksmiths, carpenters, masons, shoemakers, etc., etc. We have found the raising of stock very profitable, and can show some of the finest specimens of horse-flesh to be found on this continent, and we find a ready market for all our products. The soil is fertile and yields an abundant return for the husbandman's labor;

and, although the season is short, yet ordinarily it is long enough to ripen corn, wheat, rye, oats, and the various productions of a Northern New England or New York farm. Of late considerable attention has been paid to the cultivation of fruit trees, apples, cherries, plums, peaches, quinces, currants, gooseberries, strawberries, etc., and they are doing well, and in a few years we doubt not will be quite profitable. It is a mistaken idea that many have, that fruit trees and vines cannot be cultivated to advantage on account of the severity of the climate; I have raised as delicious sweet potatoes on my farm as I ever saw in Kentucky, and as good a crop of tobacco and hemp.

We have at the present time a large number of settlements, and connected with these are schools at which our children are being taught the ordinary branches of an English education. We are a peaceable people, living at peace among ourselves and with our white neighbors, and I believe the day is not far distant when we shall take a very respectable rank among the subjects of her majesty, the excellent and most gracious Queen of England and the Canadas. Even now, the condition and prospects of a majority of the fugitive slaves in Canada is vastly superior to that of most of the free people of color in the Northern States; and if thousands who are hanging about at the corners of streets waiting for a job, or who are mending old clothes, or blacking boots in damp cellars in Boston, New York, and other large cities, would but come among us and bring their little ones and settle down upon our fine lands, it would be but a few years before they would find themselves surrounded by a pleasant and profitable home, and their children growing up around them with every advantage for a good education, and fitting themselves for lives of usefulness and happiness. The climate is good, the soil is good, the laws protect us from molestation; each and all may sit under their own vine and fig tree with none to molest or make them afraid. We are a temperate people; it is a rare sight to see an intoxicated colored man in Canada.

My task is done, if what I have written shall inspire a deeper interest in my race, and shall lead to corresponding activity in their behalf I shall feel amply repaid.

ENDNOTES

INTRODUCTION

[1] Stowe, Harriet Beecher. *The Key to Uncle Tom's Cabin.* Boston: Jewett (1854).

[2] Hartgrove, W. B. "The Story of Josiah Henson." *The Journal of Negro History,* 3:1 (1918): 1–21.

[3] Doyle, Mary Ellen. "Josiah Henson's Narrative: Before and After." Negro American Literature Forum, 1 (1974): 176.

[4] Wallace, Maurice O. "'Are We Men?': Prince Hall, Martin Delany, and the Masculine Ideal in Black Freemasonry, 1775–1865." *American Literary History,* 9:3 (1997): 396.

SUGGESTED READING

ANDREWS, WILLIAM L. *To Tell a Free Story: The First Century of Afro-American Autobiography, 1760–1865.* Chicago: University of Illinois Press, 1988.

CASH, W. J. *The Mind of the South.* New York: Vintage, 1991.

DAVIS, CHARLES T., AND HENRY LOUIS GATES, JR., EDS. *The Slave's Narrative.* New York: Oxford, 1985.

DOUGLASS, FREDERICK. *The Narrative of the Life of Frederick Douglass.* Ed. William L. Andrews and William S. McFeely. New York: Norton, 1996.

DUBOIS, W. E. B. *The Souls of Black Folk.* Ed. Henry Louis Gates, Jr. and Terri Hume Oliver. New York: Norton, 1999.

EQUIANO, OLAUDIAH. *Narrative of the Life of Olaudiah Equiano.* New York: Barnes & Noble, 2005.

JACOBS, HARRIET. *Incidents in the Life of a Slave Girl.* Ed. Frances Smith Foster and Nellie Y. McKay. New York: Norton, 2000.

NICHOLS, WILLIAM W. "Slave Narratives: Dismissed Evidence in the Writing of Southern History." *Phylon,* 32:4 (1971): 403–409.

OLNEY, JAMES. "'I Was Born': Slave Narratives, Their Status as Autobiography and as Literature." *Callaloo,* 20 (1984): 46–73.

PRATT, LLOYD PRESLEY. "Progress, Labor, Revolution: The Modern Times of Antebellum African American Life Writing." *Novel: A Forum on Fiction,* 34:1 (2000): 55–76.

STEPTO, ROBERT. *From Behind the Veil: A Study of Afro-American Narrative.* 2nd Sub ed. Chicago: University of Illinois Press, 1991.

STOWE, HARRIET BEECHER. *Uncle Tom's Cabin.* Ed. Elizabeth Ammons. New York: Norton, 1994.

WILSON, HARRIET E. *Our Nig: Or, Sketches from the Life of a Free Black.* New York: Vintage, 1983.

Look for the following titles, available now from
The Barnes & Noble Library of Essential Reading.

Visit your Barnes & Noble bookstore,
or shop online at *www.bn.com/loer*

NONFICTION

Age of Reason, The	Thomas Paine	0760778957
Age of Revolution, The	Winston S. Churchill	0760768595
Alexander	Theodore Ayrault Dodge	0760773491
American Indian Stories	Zitkala-Ša	0760765502
Ancient Greek Historians, The	J. B. Bury	0760776350
Annals of Imperial Rome, The	Tacitus	0760788898
Antichrist, The	Friedrich Nietzsche	0760777705
Autobiography of Benjamin Franklin, The	Benjamin Franklin	0760768617
Autobiography of Charles Darwin, The	Charles Darwin	0760769087
Babylonian Life and History	E. A. Wallis Budge	0760765499
Beyond the Pleasure Principle	Sigmund Freud	0760774919
Birth of Britain, The	Winston S. Churchill	0760768579
Birth of Tragedy, The	Friedrich Nietzsche	0760780862
Century of Dishonor, A	Helen Hunt Jackson	0760778973
Characters and Events of Roman History	Guglielmo Ferrero	0760765928
Chemical History of a Candle, The	Michael Faraday	0760765227
City of God, The	Saint Augustine	0760779023
Civil War, The	Julius Caesar	0760768943
Common Law, The	Oliver Wendell Holmes	0760754985
Confessions	Jean-Jacques Rousseau	0760773599
Conquest of Gaul, The	Julius Caesar	0760768951

Consolation of Philosophy, The	Boethius	0760769796
Conversations with Socrates	Xenophon	0760770441
Creative Evolution	Henri Bergson	0760765480
Critique of Judgment	Immanuel Kant	0760762023
Critique of Practical Reason	Immanuel Kant	0760760942
Critique of Pure Reason	Immanuel Kant	0760755949
Dark Night of the Soul, The	St. John of the Cross	0760765871
De Anima	Aristotle	0760780773
Democracy and Education	John Dewey	0760765863
Democracy in America	Alexis de Tocqueville	0760752303
Descent of Man and Selection in Relation to Sex, The	Charles Darwin	0760763119
Dialogues concerning Natural Religion	David Hume	0760777713
Diary from Dixie, A	Mary Boykin Chesnut	0760779031
Discourse on Method	René Descartes	0760756023
Discourses on Livy	Niccolò Machiavelli	0760771731
Dolorous Passion of Our Lord Jesus Christ, The	Anne Catherine Emmerich	0760771715
Early History of Rome, The	Titus Livy	0760770239
Ecce Homo	Friedrich Nietzsche	0760777721
Egyptian Book of the Dead, The	E. A. Wallis Budge	0760768382
Elements, The	Euclid	0760763127
Emile	Jean-Jacques Rousseau	0760773513
Encheiridion	Epictetus	0760770204
Enquiry concerning Human Understanding, An	David Hume	0760755922
Essay Concerning Human Understanding, An	John Locke	0760760497
Essays, The	Francis Bacon	0760770182
Essence of Christianity, The	Ludwig Feuerbach	076075764X
Ethics and On the Improvement of the Understanding	Benedict de Spinoza	0760768374
Evidence as to Man's Place in Nature	Thomas H. Huxley	0760783381
Evolution and Ethics	Thomas H. Huxley	0760783373
Expression of the Emotions in Man and Animals, The	Charles Darwin	0760780803
Extraordinary Popular Delusions and the Madness of Crowds	Charles Mackay	0760755825
Fall of Troy, The	Quintus of Smyrna	0760768366
Fifteen Decisive Battles of the Western World	Edward Shepherd Creasy	0760754950
Florentine History	Niccolò Machiavelli	0760756015

Treatise of Human Nature, A	David Hume	0760771723
Trial and Death of Socrates, The	Plato	0760762007
Twelve Years a Slave	Solomon Northup	0760783349
Up From Slavery	Booker T. Washington	0760752346
Utilitarianism	John Stuart Mill	0760771758
Vindication of the Rights of Woman, A	Mary Wollstonecraft	0760754942
Voyage of the *Beagle*, The	Charles Darwin	0760754969
Wealth of Nations, The	Adam Smith	0760757615
Wilderness Hunter, The	Theodore Roosevelt	0760756031
Will to Believe and Human Immortality, The	William James	0760770190
Will to Power, The	Friedrich Nietzsche	0760777772
Worst Journey in the World, The	Aspley Cherry-Garrard	0760757593

FICTION AND LITERATURE

Abbott, Edwin A.	Flatland	0760755876
Austen, Jane	Love and Freindship	0760768560
Braddon, Mary Elizabeth	Lady Audley's Secret	0760763046
Bronte, Charlotte	Professor, The	0760768854
Burroughs, Edgar Rice	Land that Time Forgot, The	0760768862
Burroughs, Edgar Rice	Martian Tales Trilogy, The	076075585X
Butler, Samuel	Way of All Flesh, The	0760765855
Castiglione, Baldesar	Book of the Courtier, The	0760768323
Cather, Willa	Alexander's Bridge	0760768870
Cather, Willa	One of Ours	0760777683
Chaucer, Geoffrey	Troilus and Criseyde	0760768919
Chesterton, G. K.	Ball and the Cross, The	0760783284
Chesterton, G. K.	Innocence and Wisdom of Father Brown, The	0760773556
Chesterton, G. K.	Man Who Was Thursday, The	0760763100
Childers, Erskine	Riddle of the Sands, The	0760765235
Cleland, John	Fanny Hill	076076591X
Conrad, Joseph	Secret Agent, The	0760783217
Cooper, James Fenimore	Pioneers, The	0760779015
Cummings, E. E.	Enormous Room, The	076077904X
Defoe, Daniel	Journal of the Plague Year, A	0760752370
Dos Passos, John	Three Soldiers	0760757542
Doyle, Arthur Conan	Complete Brigadier Gerard, The	0760768897
Doyle, Arthur Conan	Lost World, The	0760755833
Doyle, Arthur Conan	White Company and Sir Nigel, The	0760768900

THE BARNES & NOBLE
LIBRARY OF ESSENTIAL READING

This series has been established to provide affordable access to books of literary, academic, and historic value—works of both well-known writers and those who deserve to be rediscovered. Selected and introduced by scholars and specialists with an intimate knowledge of the works, these volumes present complete, original texts in a modern, readable typeface—welcoming a new generation of readers to influential and important books of the past. With more than 300 titles already in print and more than 100 forthcoming, the Library of Essential Reading offers an unrivaled variety of thought, scholarship, and entertainment. Best of all, these handsome and durable paperbacks are priced to be exceptionally affordable. For a full list of titles, visit *www.bn.com/loer*.